LUCIFER'S QUEST

Undoing Babel

Dr. David A. Rice
with
Kim Chadwell

LUCIFER'S QUEST Undoing Babel
By David A. Rice
ISBN: 9781795827751
Copyright © **2019**
All Rights Reserved.

All Scripture sources are marked inline

Cover design
by
Classie Powell

David A. Rice
Website: https://promusement.live/

Printed in the United States of America
First Printing: January 2019

CONTENTS

Kim Chadwell

Known as "Today's Esther" Kim is the author of Dripping in Grace and founder of Kim Chadwell Ministries, a ministry dedicated to training, education and support for the poor. From orphaned to owned, Kim has turned tragedy to triumph showing how everyone, with God's grace, can grow and live in the fulness of happiness. Kim's prophetic words have been heard throughout the world.

This book is dedicated to Cathy:
God's child,
the nicest lady I have ever known,
the mother of my children,
my wife.

It was also given to him to make war with the saints and to overcome them, and authority over every tribe and people and tongue and nation was given to him. (Revelation 13:7)

"But the one who endures to the end, he will be saved." (Matthew 24:13)

PROLOGUE

I am not a prophet. This book is based on years of study. I am a student, an observer, and a Watchman on the Wall.

I have given Scripture and I've given strong arguments. I sometimes offer two, possible future scenarios, which may even contradict each other. Meaning, they are exactly what I say that they are: *possible scenarios.* I also admit I could be wrong.

This book contains a great number of topics and perspective that represent what I believe. I can be highly opinionated. Some are comfortable with my strong opinions, others not so much. Nonetheless, I believe what I believe. I hope that I do not come across too strongly.

I am not a prophet. I do not know the future. I like you am watching. Jesus said to watch. This is all the reason that I need.

Whatever comes to pass over the next few months and years, it doesn't look good for the Bible Believing Child of God.

It should be a rip-roaring good time for the Dominionist…

…but for the ones clinging to the cross, it may be very rough.

David A Rice

"Behold, they are one people, and they all have the same language. And this is what they began to do, and now nothing which they purpose to do will be impossible for them..." —Jehovah God

PART ONE

THE PAST

INCIDENT AT BABEL

That Which God Has Separated...

As a child, I remember learning about the Tower of Babel in Sunday School. The illustrations showed drawings of a somewhat circular, slightly crooked, large tower. It had a ramp as large as a road circling around it from bottom to top. It showed the tower still under construction, still unfinished, of course, with workers hurrying up and down the ramp. I am not certain if those drawings and illustrations were realistic or not. I have found no description of the tower itself written by an eyewitness who observed its construction. However, the above description is probably as good of a guess as any.

1 Now the whole earth used the same language and the same words. 2 It came about as they journeyed east, that they found a plain in the land of Shinar and settled there. 3 They said to one another, "Come, let us make bricks and burn them thoroughly." And they used brick for stone, and they used tar for mortar. 4 They said, "Come, let us build for ourselves a city, and a tower whose top will reach into heaven, and let us make for ourselves a name, otherwise we will be scattered abroad over the face of the whole earth." 5 The Lord came down to see the city and the tower which the sons of men had built. 6 The Lord said, "Behold, they are one people, and they all have the same language. And this is what they began to do, and now nothing which they purpose to do will be impossible for them. 7 Come, let Us go down and there confuse their language, so that they will not understand one another's speech." 8 So the Lord scattered them abroad from there over the face of the whole earth; and they stopped building the city. 9 Therefore its

name was called Babel, because there the Lord confused the language of the whole earth; and from there the Lord scattered them abroad over the face of the whole earth. (Genesis 11:1-9 NASB)

I remember as a teenager I would listen to men talk about World War II. To me, as I listened, it seemed like ancient history. To the men it was a memory which would never fade. Nowadays, if I talk about the Vietnam War, my children are bored. For me, as I grew up, the Vietnam War was very serious, and coverage of the war was on TV almost every night. In 1969, at eighteen years of age, I joined the Army. They sent me to Germany, not Vietnam, for which I am grateful, but some of the young men I trained with died in that war. I will never forget Vietnam. For me, World War II is ancient history, but I will never forget the Vietnam War. To my children World War II, and the Vietnam War are just very old stories.

The same is true of ancient times. For the people who reached the plains of Shinar the flood of Noah was ancient history. The younger generations heard about the flood. Some of the Elders remembered and told the story of prior sins and what it had cost mankind. The new generation felt the old story no longer mattered; it was a *new* generation. There were thousands of people and the vast majority were without memory of the flood or the days that followed. These people, this new generation, saw beautiful rainbows yet thought little of their meaning.

For them, it was difficult to even imagine a time when there had been neither rain nor vibrant rainbows. This new generation knew little of the previous disaster. The place was new. Everything was new.

Imagine that you were there...

All seemed to have jobs...there was plenty of work. Bartering was a thing of the past. King Nimrod had introduced money and the new coins created a wonderful exchange system. You could buy food grown on farms without leaving your neighborhood and you could buy most anything at the market. Workers had Saturday off and the clubs did a rousing business on Friday nights. If you didn't have your own business, jobs were easy to find. Construction was everywhere. You could find a job building houses or on the construction of the new Temple.

The new Temple was a sight to see! Ordinary buildings and homes were mostly single-story structures. The city wall was high, and you could see it from almost anywhere, but that Temple, WOW! You could see it from anywhere. It rose higher every day. It was almost like a living thing... you could watch it grow... King Nimrod announced the temple was going to reach into the Heavens where God lived. Word on the street was that Nimrod was training an army to fight Jehovah and his angels! That would be some fight!

It happened on a Thursday. No one, ever, had to ask *which* Thursday; everyone knew *which* Thursday. That Thursday morning began just like any other day. You woke up, washed, dressed, and had fried oxtail with goat milk for breakfast. You left as usual to go to work. But outside, it was utter chaos. You couldn't get to work. The streets were full of confused, frustrated, angry people... You went over and found your best friend, but when you said good morning and asked him what was going on, he looked at you like you were crazy... When he answered you, it was unintelligible... pure nonsense. You soon realized that the whole world had gone crazy.

Running home, you found you could still talk with your own family. Your uncles, aunts and cousins could still communicate, but everybody else had lost it! So, you packed up your stuff and left town. There were no roads and you didn't know where you were going. You only knew that you had to get out of there.

As you were leaving, you found another family, and then another who spoke your language. You formed a big group. Soon, there were almost a thousand people in your group. You saw other groups but there was this deep fear. You were afraid of them and they were afraid of you. When you came to the river, they turned one way and your group the other.

Egypt: Let's keep this imaginary journey going…

The ground got dryer. The sun got hotter. The rains had stopped but there was mud and water down by the big river. You pitched your tents near the water and planted your grain in the mud. Harvest had been a panic that first year. Just as they were beginning to bring in the grain, the river started to get bigger. You had never seen anything like this. It doubled almost overnight and then again and again. Soon all the land where the crops had been planted was under water. You had to move your tent five times that year… twice in one night. That was something you would never forget, but it was just an old story to your children and their children.

Continuing our little tale…

A large city was built. The city is named, "City of The King." It also had a new temple under construction. But this temple was different. It looked like the old pyramids that had survived the flood. Not so big or so grand perhaps, but it was huge. They said if the king were buried in that temple he would live forever! The King wasn't even old or near death, but there was great pressure to finish it within his lifetime.

Someone had named the new nation *Egypt*. It had a certain ring to it…Egypt… Egypt … Egypt. Egypt was an excellent name.

Then, the other group with a different language suddenly liked your city. They couldn't even speak Egyptian, but they wanted to take everything you had built and chase you out! There was war, but they lost. Now, the other group lived in the slums just outside of town. It would now be they who would build the Temple. Life became easier.

There was talk that the Pharaoh (*"king"* in Egyptian) was going to conquer the entire world and make everyone speak Egyptian.

End of the imaginary journey…

A Single Goal

Throughout all of history, this has been the constant goal: one language, one ruler, one government, one nation. The pattern has continued: a thousand madmen starting as many wars... Greece, Rome, the Ottomans, Great Britain, Nazi Germany, the United States of America. In each place, and at each time, there were madmen, and their followers, who wanted to rule the world. Some of these people live in Washington D.C. today, pushing for Global Governance.

Lucifer's quest is always trying to undo what God did at Babel.

HISTORY OF THE TOWER OF BABEL
ACCORDING TO THE ANCIENT BOOK OF JASHER*

Phut Mitzraim   Cush Canaan

King Nimrod and his four princes decide to build a great city with a tower to reach heaven.

600,000 men assemble for construction.

The 600,000 divide into three groups.
Group 1: Plan to ascend to heaven and fight God.
Group 2: Plan to ascend to heaven to place their own gods there.
Group 3: Plan to ascend and strike God with bows and arrows.

They built a mighty tower which took one year to reach the top. The climb was done daily without stop for many days and years.

* Johnson, Ken, Th.D. *Ancient Book of Jasher*, United States: 2008 21-22

12

As Punishment:

God sends seventy angels to strike them with confusion of languages.

Group 1: God scatters them throughout the earth.
Group 2: God marks them black and white colored*.
Group 3: God kills them and they also kill each other.

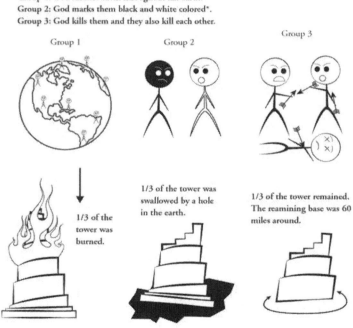

Group 1   Group 2   Group 3

1/3 of the tower was burned.

1/3 of the tower was swallowed by a hole in the earth.

1/3 of the tower remained. The reamining base was 60 miles around.

60x3 =180 The original tower base was 180 miles in circumference.

*It is unknown if they were stuck black and white individually or a multi-colored marking.

Dr. David A. Rice, with, Kim Chadwell

CONSPIRACY HISTORY

"You belong to your father, the devil, and you want to carry out your father's desires. He was a murderer from the beginning, not holding to the truth, for there is no truth in him. When he lies, he speaks his native language, for he is a liar and the father of lies." (John 8:44)

There are two competing views of history: The Accidental, and, The Conspiratorial.

The Accidental Theory:

Simply put, the Accidental Theory maintains that the buildup and fall of nations, wars and their winners and losers, financial upturns and downturns, are all the product of unplanned accidents.

The Conspiratorial Theory:

The Conspiratorial Theory maintains that there are wealthy and powerful men in the world who sit down and plan these events to their own benefit. These men, often referred to as the Illuminati, are above governments, cause conflict, sell arms to both sides, and offer resolutions to problems that they themselves have caused... but solutions always come with a price.

The Conspiratorial View of history is the one which makes the most sense to me. This view is bolstered by the existence of plans written long before many of the events ever took place. One of the strongest examples is a letter written by Albert Pike describing a vision, which he penned in a letter to Mazzini, (an Occultist, Italian politician and leader of the movement to unify Italy) dated August 15, 1871. This letter graphically outlined plans for three world wars seen as necessary to bring about the New World Order. We can marvel at how accurately it has predicted events that have now already taken place.

We no longer have the original letter; however, we do have multiple quotes from the original which predate the first world war. Some have protested that the letter does not exist. However, quotes from a lost document, obtained from several different sources, are enough to prove that it did exist, and contents are established by agreement of quotes. This is acceptable proof in a court of law, however I cannot say, with absolute certainty, that it ever existed but I believe that it did.

The following are quotes found in documents supposedly dated prior to 1910:

"The Third World War must be fomented by taking advantage of the differences caused by the "Agentur" of the "Illuminati" between the political Zionists and the leaders of Islamic World. The war must be conducted in such a way that Islam (the Moslem Arabic World) and political Zionism (the State of Israel) mutually destroy each other. Meanwhile the other nations, once more divided on this issue, will be constrained to fight to the point of complete physical, moral, spiritual and economical exhaustion. We shall unleash the Nihilists and the atheists, and we shall provoke a formidable social cataclysm which in all its horror, will show clearly to the nations the effect of absolute atheism, origin of savagery and of the most bloody turmoil. Then everywhere, the citizens, obliged to defend themselves against the world minority of revolutionaries, will exterminate those destroyers of civilization, and the multitude, disillusioned with Christianity, whose deistic spirits will from that moment be without compass or direction, anxious for an ideal, but without knowing where to render its adoration, will receive the true light through the universal manifestation of the pure doctrine of Lucifer, brought finally out in the public view. This manifestation will result from the general reactionary movement which will follow the destruction of Christianity and atheism, both conquered and exterminated, at the same time."[i1]

If you are up to date on current events, you will understand that WWIII is forming, exactly as the Masonic Witch, Albert Pike, said it would.

Christians have long held a split view concerning Biblical history and prophecy. My original biblical education led me to believe that God had a plan that was perfect and everlasting…that God knew everything from the beginning, and He had everything under control. Lucifer, or the Devil, on the other hand, was a bumbling fool who knew nothing and had no previous knowledge of anything….he simply bounced around reacting with knee jerk reactions to the plan of God as it unfolded.

A careful reading of the Bible will tell you that God, indeed, does have a plan. But far from being an ignorant fool reacting in knee jerk fashion, Lucifer has understood God's plan from the Garden of Eden and has planned, and continues to plan, ways to defeat Jehovah and remain the god of this world.

Genesis 3: [14] So the Lord God said to the serpent, "Because you have done this,
"Cursed are you above all livestock
and all wild animals!
You will crawl on your belly
and you will eat dust
all the days of your life.
[15] And I will put enmity
between you and the woman,
and between your offspring and hers;
he will crush your head,

"Who Was Albert Pike?" WW1 - The True Cause of World War 1, www.threeworldwars.com/albert-pike2.htm.

and you will strike his heel." (NIV)

I believe that the conversation between God and Lucifer, recorded in Genesis Chapter Three, was more involved and detailed than we would understand from the short version. It is easy to believe Scripture's short synopsis—but it was a much longer event than Scripture had room for. While he certainly did not understand every detail, Lucifer seems to have come away from that conversation with a clear view of the overall plan of God, if not the details. He began immediately to create strategies that would lead to destruction of the plans and designs of God.

Genesis 6:1 When human beings began to increase in number on the earth and daughters were born to them, ² the sons of God saw that the daughters of humans were beautiful, and they married any of them they chose.³ Then the Lord said, "My Spirit will not contend with humans forever, for they are mortal; their days will be a hundred and twenty years."
⁴ The Nephilim were on the earth in those days—and also afterward—when the sons of God went to the daughters of humans and had children by them. They were the heroes of old, men of renown. (NIV)

It is true that the sons of God saw that the daughters of mankind were beautiful, and that they took any they chose as wives for themselves. But it is deeper than that. Back in Genesis three, God had told Lucifer that He would put hostility between him and the woman, and between his seed and her seed and that the Seed of the woman would strike his (Lucifer's) head, and he (Lucifer) would strike the heel of the seed of the woman.

It was not long after this verse in Genesis three that the Sons of God came down to the daughters of men and in Unholy Matrimony began to create a hybrid race of lost and unredeemable creatures known as

Nephilim. To students of the Bible they were known as the Mighty Men of Old. To the Greeks, they were known as Titans. By the time of the flood, perhaps the only pure, 100% humans left on the planet were Noah, his wife and sons.

This was a strange promise. We do not think of angels as *having seed,* but if they took wives and had children, they must. Jesus said that Angels "do not marry". This, however, speaks of a contract and not reproduction or sexual intercourse. One not so overly religious might believe that they simply have a different type of agreement or contract and not that they are either neutered or celibate.

Here in this scripture we have the s*eed of the woman* in mortal conflict with the *seed of Satan.* We know that Jesus Christ is the seed of the woman, but who, or what, is the *seed of Satan?* We will soon attempt to answer that question.

Can you see a plan here? Lucifer would someday be defeated by the seed of the woman. What if there were no humans left? With no pure humans around the promised Seed could not be born. The answer was to pollute human DNA.

Later, we find Nephilim tribes in the Promised Land. The fear of them sent Israel roaming in the wilderness for forty years. Lucifer had the baby boys killed when Moses was born and again at the time of Jesus' birth. Can you see a plan?

Today, man is playing with DNA. Scientists around the world are creating human-animal chimeras. Transhumanism has become a major field of scientific research. They plan openly for what they are calling Man 2.0. Do you see a plan?

There is no salvation for Nephilim, hybrids or chimeras. If Lucifer can rewrite the DNA of humans, he can create a race of immortal beings—beings that God himself cannot save. Beings that will worship Satan as god. Is there a plan? Is there a mark that makes one cease to be human?

God commanded the Israelites to go into the camps of the *Nephilim* and <u>kill *every* individual</u>. Scripture indicates that they failed to do so. We know that the Israelites did not get them all. Nephilim skeletons, giants with strange skulls, six fingers and six toes, have been found in Europe and the Americas. Is there seed of Lucifer still among us?

Numbers 31: [14] Moses was angry with the officers of the army—the commanders of thousands and commanders of hundreds—who returned from the battle.

[15] "Have you allowed all the women to live?" he asked them. (NIV)

We understand that all the individuals in the Nephilim tribes carried the angelic gene but not all were giants. Scripture indicates those who carried the gene were not human and could not be saved. Could it be that the giant gene died out, but the Nephilim gene remained? Does the seed of Satan walk among us? Do they now outnumber us?

"As it was in the days of Noah..."

In the days of Noah, perhaps only half a dozen pure humans remained alive. Was the gross evil of those days was among the hybrids, not the humans? Is it possible that the true believers are part of a very small remnant of pure-bred humans that remain? Could this be why there is so much evil in the world? Is this why believers are cautioned to only marry other believers? Is it possible that a believer could marry into a Nephilim family and produce children who cannot be saved?

These questions are to make you think.

The *purpose* of this book *is* to make you think!

I ask that you
open your eyes and see,
open your ears and hear,
open your mind…
and think!

Lucifer has a quest. He is undoing Babel.

CHRISTIANITY VERSUS AMERICANISM
Hiding the Cross Behind the Flag

The next few chapters may offend you. At times I am going to criticize your church and even your nation. I may debunk lies that you now hold as unquestionable truth. Please bear with me as I lay the necessary foundation. There are important truths you must understand.

First, let me say that I love both America and the Church. Without the church, I would not know Jesus. Without America, I might have never known freedom. I was personally blessed to be raised both in the church and in America. I thank God for both. But having said that, I now know I was taught a good number of lies in both the church and in school. I cannot teach new truth until we have dealt with the lies and faced the half-truths.

America was called a Christian nation because most Americans were, in general, Christians. It has been said that approximately half of the Christians in the world today are Christians because American missionaries left the blessings of America and took the Gospel to other countries. (The American *government* is a different story, as we shall soon discover.)

The Babylonian Gospel, and mixture, were the only messages I ever heard. Even five years ago, if you had asked me to tell you what I believed, much of what I said would have had its roots in Baptist Denominational Distinctives, the Masonic Religion, and the Great American Lie. Even after years abroad, where I was confronted by a Gospel not mixed with American Patriotism, much of what I believed was more American than Biblical.

I was raised a Baptist. The basics of the Gospel were preached. We would sing the right hymns. But it was all about walking the aisle, shaking the Preacher's hand, repeating a canned prayer, and getting dunked in the ornate, marble baptistry. With "Once Saved, Always Saved," as a core doctrine, what you did after baptism was relatively unimportant. A strict moral code was taught more from the Masonic point of view than Biblical Gospel. The thrust was that one needed to live right because it is good for your country, society, and community. We were taught that living right would make you healthy, wealthy and wise.

It was always assumed that if you walked the aisle, shook the preacher's hand, repeated the prayer, and got dunked, you were going to Heaven. No one dared question that formula.

Some of the old men in the church had fought in World War I. Most of the adult men had fought in World War II and/or the Korean War. The young men, off to Vietnam, often returned in a box.

No matter what the truth was about Vietnam, Korea or any other war, if you were a Christian, you supported America, the Flag and the latest war. The most ungodly, and unchristian, thing a person could do was to question America. Somehow, we *knew* that God was an American, and that America was the Kingdom of God!

The Methodists believed differently than we did about salvation. They could lose their salvation. However, they, too, thought God was an American! The Presbyterians knew it too. They knew that not only was God an American, He was a Presbyterian! Everyone agreed it was very important to be a good American. If America did it, it was God's will, and God's way!

The church services on the Fourth of July were always patriotic. The National Guard Color Guard, dressed in full military dress, holding the American Flag high, marched down the center aisle in uniformed step. The congregation stood and sang the National Anthem. Men saluted as the Color Guard stood in the front of the church with flags in hand. The pride was palpable.

At Christmas, the children would perform a Nativity play, baby Jesus in the manger, under a Christmas Tree. At Easter we would hold a Sunrise Service, followed by Sunday school with an Easter egg hunt. Then at the 11:00 am church service we would all sing "Hallelujah, He arose!" at the top of our lungs…

There was always mixture. There were always things that had to be emphasized and things that could not be taught. My Grandfather was a 33rd Degree Mason and a "Lifetime Deacon" down at the Baptist Church. I do not know how many of the men on that board were Master Masons, but I would imagine that it was a clear majority. This was an upscale church… a church where the Rich and Famous could feel at home.

It was my Grandfather and his Masonic buddies who planned the new Sanctuary as a Greek Temple, designed and built with strict Masonic Architecture, based on ancient Egyptian magic. The result was a building that looked like a Masonic Temple with a steeple and a cross stuck on top.

Mixture on Display

But then I left home, and I went off and became Pentecostal! I spoke in tongues, prophesied, and saw real miracles. But the Pentecostals were also sold on the American Way, Christmas Trees and Easter Bunnies. More than that, they were frightened and legalistic to the max. I could tell how spiritual a man was by looking at his wife. If she wore dresses to the floor, kept her head covered, and wore neither jewelry nor makeup…that was one Holy and Righteous man! But an odd question continually surfaced with the Pentecostals, "If I get in an accident and I say a bad word, and I die before I can repent, will I go to Hell?" I sometimes found these people most unpleasant...

Over the last twenty years I have watched Pentecostals go through a great change. They started a rapid flight away from legalism. Unfortunately, most of them passed the Truth going ninety miles an hour and slid right into what some have called sloppy agape. The current approved term is *Hyper-Grace.* This is now a politicly correct religion... You preach on the importance of accepting everybody and offending no one. You NEVER preach on sin or call for repentance. Scripture read aloud and sermons to be preached are scrutinized ahead of time. If a verse could possibly offend someone, it is not read. If there is an offensive phrase or word in a sermon, it is scratched out and never spoken. Only happy scripture and happy sermons are allowed.

Altar-calls are for happy prophecy, blessings, and miracles. They are NEVER for repentance or salvation. Oh, and it no longer matters what you wear! As a single man, a very long time ago, I saw pole dancers better dressed than some of the young ladies I now see in church.

Thank God there are numerous exceptions to the rule and godly churches do exist.

But, still the lie of American patriotism pervades the American Church. You cannot be a good Christian if you are not a strong patriot. You cannot have a cross unless it is draped with the American flag.

"President Trump must be from God..."
"America and the Kingdom of God are one and the same..."
"Surely Trump is a Prince, sent from God to save God's Country."
(in her sin, and grant her time and freedom to sin some more...)
"God is American and Jesus lounges around Heaven in red, white and blue pajamas..."

You may think those statements extreme, but I have seen these remarks, made by Christians, in posts and comments on social media.

Jesus asked, *"When the Son of Man comes, will He find faith on earth?" (Luke 18:8)* I am leaning more and more to the negative reply... "No, none, or very little."

If, with a prayerful attitude, you throw out everything you were taught, and *read the Bible*, you will find that the Bible is very simple and straight-forward. You will discover that America is not the Kingdom of God, but rather Babylon, Jesus is nothing like what you always thought He was and being a Christian has little or nothing to do with walking an aisle, shaking a Preacher's hand, repeating a little prayer and getting dunked in a baptistry... *not even an ornate, marble baptistry...*

Let us contrast two strong, foundational statements:

We hold these truths to be self-evident, that all men are created equal, that they are endowed by their Creator with certain unalienable Rights, that among these are Life, Liberty and the pursuit of Happiness.

The person who loves father or mother more than Me is not worthy of Me; the person who loves son or daughter more than Me is not worthy of Me. And whoever doesn't take up his cross and follow Me is not worthy of Me. Anyone finding his life will lose it, and anyone losing his life because of Me will find it.

When I was in High School, the State of Florida mandated a course called Americanism Vs. Communism. In that class we learned about the wonderful American heroes: Washington, Jefferson, Franklin, and the like. We also learned about the terrible tyrants of communism: Lenin, Stalin, and Mao. We diligently studied all the reasons the American system of Government works, and how communism never will.

What I would like to give you is a different kind of course; a course which should be mandated by the Board of Education of the Kingdom of Heaven, for *every* Kingdom Citizen living as a foreigner and alien in the United States of America: a course in Christianity Vs. Americanism, or perhaps we should call it: Kingdom Principles Vs. Americanism.

Let us contrast the two systems:

1.) The Kingdom of God and

2.) The United States of America.

Older American Christians were taught, both by their Pastors and the school system, that the United States and the Kingdom of God are synonymous. You cannot be a good American unless you live like a Christian. If you are a Christian, you must be a good American.

Somehow, the men in the great American seminaries, decided and taught for over two hundred years that these two statements could be reconciled. You could believe that your Creator had given you a right to life, but you could not be worthy of Jesus if you found your life. You were not worthy if you did not die to yourself and lose your life (and rights) for his sake. So, your Creator gave you a right to life and your God took it away. This will make you scratch your head.

The full statement in the Declaration of Independence is:

"We hold these truths to be self-evident, that all men are created equal, that they are endowed by their Creator with certain unalienable Rights, that among these are Life, Liberty and the pursuit of Happiness. — That to secure these rights, Governments are instituted among Men, deriving their just powers from the consent of the governed..."

Deism

The Creator created, then abandoned the world, having established "Governments" to run everything!

Please study the doctrine of the Deists. This is a core and absolute belief in Deism!

"The term deism refers not to a specific religion but rather to a particular perspective on the nature of God. Deists believe that a single creator god does exist, but they take their evidence from reason and logic, not the revelatory acts and miracles that form the basis of faith in many organized religions. Deists hold that after the motions of the

universe were set in place, God retreated and had no further interaction with the created universe or the beings within it."[ii2]

[2] Beyer, Catherine, et al. "Deists Believe in One God Who Is Impersonal." *Thoughtco.*, Dotdash, www.thoughtco.com/deism-95703.

The Bible:

Paul frequently speaks of himself as a slave to Jesus Christ.

Scripture says:

"All who are under the yoke as slaves must regard their own masters to be worthy of all respect, so that God's name and His teaching will not be blasphemed. Those who have believing masters should not be disrespectful to them because they are brothers, but should serve them better, since those who benefit from their service are believers and dearly loved.

Teach and encourage these things. If anyone teaches other doctrine and does not agree with the sound teaching of our Lord Jesus Christ and with the teaching that promotes godliness, he is conceited, understanding nothing, but has a sick interest in disputes and arguments over words. From these come envy, quarreling, slander, evil suspicions, and constant disagreement among people whose minds are depraved and deprived of the truth, who imagine that godliness is a way to material gain.

But godliness with contentment is a great gain. For we brought nothing into the world, and we can take nothing out. But if we have food and clothing, we will be content with these.

But those who want to be rich fall into temptation, a trap, and many foolish and harmful desires, which plunge people into ruin and destruction. For the love of money is a root of all kinds of evil, and by craving it, some have wandered away from the faith and pierced themselves with many pains. (1 Timothy 6:1-10)

Try preaching that to your favorite Trump supporter!

The Declaration of Independence:

The Declaration of Independence states that your Creator has given you an "unalienable right" to liberty. Scripture says that you must give up everything, deny yourself, and follow Christ. The Declaration of

Independence states that your Creator has given you an immutable, unchangeable, permanent and forever right to seek happiness.

According to the wisdom of the American Church there is no problem here. *Perhaps you are smarter than the American Church?*

The consistent message in America, and the message that got Donald Trump elected is:

"Every American has the right to a good job, good pay, and all the "stuff" he could ever desire!"

Many in the American Church have awakened to the fact that those wonderful statements in the Declaration of Independence are the doctrines of demons and the principles of Babylon. Unfortunately, most Christians do not have a clue.

It was Satan who offered Jesus the riches of this world's kingdoms. Satan rebelled against God because he wanted to be free. The Devil's sales pitch has *always* been to offer freedom, riches and knowledge...

Always... from the very beginning.

The serpent said to the woman, "You surely will not die! For God knows that in the day you eat from it your eyes will be opened, and you will be like God, knowing good and evil." Genesis 3: 4,5

He [Satan]said to Him, "All these things I will give You, if You fall down and worship me." Matthew 4:9

It was God who separated men by tribes and tongues and nations. Babel was, outside of the cross of Jesus Christ, the greatest blow ever dealt to Satan and the Kingdoms of this world.

God had said:

"If they have begun to do this as one people all having the same language, then nothing they plan to do will be impossible for them. Come, let Us go down there and confuse their language so that they will not understand one another's speech." So, from there the Lord scattered them over the face of the whole earth, and they stopped building the city. Therefore its name is called Babel for there the Lord confused the language of the whole earth, and from there the Lord scattered them over the face of the whole earth. (Genesis 11)

I will keep repeating: "nothing *they* (fallen man under Lucifer) plan to do will be impossible for them!" This is why God divided and separated people into groups. Satan wanted to defeat God and establish himself as the god of this world, forever. He still does.

The United States is a *guinea pig*, a trial…the Babylonian forerunner…to the New World Order. What America has been on a single continent the New World Order / Kingdom of the Beast will be on a global scale. This is the Devil's plan. Having reunited the world, he will take on God at Armageddon and win, becoming the god of this world for all of eternity. This is Lucifer's plan and he has just enough ego and pride to believe his own stuff.

Dr. David A. Rice, with, Kim Chadwell

Mottos of Rebellion:
"Ordo Ab Chao" or *"Order Out of Chaos."* What chaos? The chaos created by God at Babylon!

What is the cry of America?
"Give me your poor; your huddled masses…"

Mottos on the Dollar:
"E Pluribus Unum" *Out of Many, One.*
"Annuit cœptis" *He [?] has favoured our undertakings.*
"Novus ordo seclorum" *New World Order*
"IN GOD WE TRUST" *(Placed between the Egyptian pyramid with the all-seeing eye of Osiris, & the Phoenix.)*

E Pluribus Unum speaks to undoing divisions established by God at Babel.
Annuit cœptis simply says that Lucifer has favoured our undertakings.
Novus Ordo Seclorum is officially translated as *"New Order of the Ages."* Or, simply put, *"New World Order."*

Placing the motto **IN GOD WE TRUST** between the symbols of the pagan god Osiris and a phoenix, gives us insight that the Masonic-controlled Evangelical Churches in America were determined we should never see.

34

According to Richard S. Patterson and Richardson Dougall:
*"**Annuit coeptis**" meaning "favor our undertakings," along with the motto on the reverse of the Great Seal, "**Novus ordo seclorum**,"meaning "new order of the ages" can both be traced to lines by the Roman poet Virgil. "Annuit cœptis" comes from the Aeneid, book IX, line 625. It is a prayer by Ascanius, the son of the hero of the story Aeneas. "Iuppiter omnipotens, audacibus adnue coeptis." Translated: "Jupiter [Satan] Almighty, favour [my] bold undertakings." Said just before slaying an enemy warrior, Remulus.[3]*

---

[3] I Golden Screen Cinemas,
ipfs.io/ipfs/QmXoypizjW3WknFiJnKLwHCnL72vedxjQkDDP1mXWo6uco/wiki/Annuit
_coeptis.html.

"E Pluribus Unum," speaks to undoing the divisions…established by God, at Babel.

AMERICA AND ISRAEL THE CONNECTION:

I would be remiss if I failed to mention Israel, like the United States of America, chose the curse and not the blessing.

While speaking about America we must pay attention to the connection of America with Israel and the Jews. Jonathan Cahn, a well-known Rabbi and teacher, has written several books on this subject. I don't want to repeat his work, but the subject must be addressed. The shear amount of negative garbage on social media concerning this good Rabbi is enough to tell me he is doing something right. I highly recommend his work.

Two Camps:

I find people divided into two camps regarding the America-Israel connection. Some insist that because of the Babylonian connection there can be no connection of America to Israel. Others in the opposite camp insist that America is Israel and therefore cannot be Babylon.

I sit between the camps and insist that while America is indeed the Babylon of the End-Times, America does have a strong and historic connection to Israel and the Jews. As a matter of fact, America's eventual destruction is aimed at both the Babylonian connection and the Israeli connection.

CONNECTION ONE

The first connection between the United States and Israel comes through Christopher Columbus. You probably know that, "In 1492, Columbus sailed the ocean blue." But there is more to the story.

Early in 1492 Boabdil, the last of the Moorish rulers, surrendered the keys of Granada. Columbus was a personal eyewitness to this surrender. The long war against the Moors had ended and now the energies of the kingdom could be directed outward. The Prior to the Dominican convent of La Rábida, Father Juan Perez, the confessor of the queen was impressed by Columbus. Perez spoke to the Queen, and she influenced the king.

These are the first words written in the diary of Christopher Columbus:

"In the same month in which their Majesties [Ferdinand and Isabella] issued the edict that all Jews should be driven out of the kingdom and its territories, in the same month they gave me the order to undertake with sufficient men my expedition of discovery to the Indies."

So begins Christopher Columbus's diary.

The expulsion Columbus refers to in his diary was a cataclysmic event in 1492. On July 30, 1492 the entire Jewish community, some 200,000 people, were expelled from Spain. The year 1492 has been almost as important to Jewish history as in American history.[4]

In the last days of the expulsion, rumors spread throughout Spain that the fleeing refugees had swallowed gold and diamonds, and many Jews were knifed to death by brigands hoping to find treasures in their

---

[4] "Modern Jewish History: The Spanish Expulsion." *Suleyman*, www.jewishvirtuallibrary.org/the-spanish-expulsion-1492.

stomachs. In some instances, Spanish ship Captains charged Jewish passengers exorbitant sums then dumped them overboard in the middle of the ocean. Thousands of Jews died while trying to reach safety.

1492 was an earth-shaking year:

- The Jewish community in Spain was the largest in the world.
- Islam was beaten, and Catholicism reigned supreme.
- Father Juan Perez got Columbus in front of the King.
- The Jews were given thirty days to convert or leave Spain.
- The Government confiscated all the wealth and property of the Jews.
- The King used the money from the Jews to finance the voyage of Columbus.
- Columbus discovered America.
- America would become the next safe-haven and home for the Jews.

CONNECTION TWO

The second connection between America and Israel is found in the fact that the majority of the first European immigrants to settle in the New World were born again, Bible believing Christians. These Christians, according to Scripture, had been grafted onto the vine and were spiritual descendants of Abraham. These Pilgrims even called the place, "New Israel," and tried to make Hebrew the official language of their colony.

CONNECTION THREE

The third connection between the United States and Israel is that George Washington connected the United States to Israel on the day of the nation's founding. Although he himself was a Deist and not a Christian, Washington stood in a tiny church in New York City and led the first Congress in prayer and vows to God and dedicates the nation to the God of Abraham. That little church building in New York City, where those solemn vows were made, still stands today. It survived the attacks of 9/11, and remains standing; standing at Ground Zero, as a testimony of those vows.

America, like Israel, was founded on the Word of God and dedicated to the God of the Word. Like Israel, we have broken our vows and we have rebelled against God and his Word. Like Israel, we have sinned. Like Israel, we kill our children, offering them to Baal on the altar of convenience. We recoil in horror at the thought that the Israelites would throw their babies into the fire, but we officially sanction allowing babies to be partially born and allowing an abortionist to insert a needle into their heads, suck out their brains and collapse their skulls. This act is a right sanctified and guaranteed by the Government of the United States.

CONNECTION FOUR

The fourth connection between America and Israel is that both countries are connected through a scripture in the old testament, 2 Chronicles 7:14. No verse, in all of Scripture, has been quoted more and claimed by more Christians for America more than this single verse.

[If] My people who are called by My name shall humble themselves and pray and seek My face and turn from their wicked ways, then I will hear from heaven, I will forgive their sin and will heal their land. (2Chronicles7:14.)

What American Christian has not heard this verse ad nauseum?

Let us here do what almost no one ever does, let us *look* at this verse *in context.*

12 Then the Lord appeared to Solomon at night and said to him, "I have heard your prayer and have chosen this place for Myself as a house of sacrifice. (NASB)

This is at the dedication of Solomon's Temple in Israel. God says that He has heard their prayer and that He has accepted that place as a place of sacrifice.

Next, God makes a statement that would shock and sicken many American Christians, and pastors, should they ever read it. In a religious environment where all good things are credited to God, and everything bad attributed to the Devil, this verse should leave many Christians with their heads under their pillow, trembling…

13 If I shut up the heavens so that there is no rain, or if I command the locust to devour the land, or if I send pestilence among My people,

Then comes the verse American Christians have claimed as their own...

14 and if My people who are called by My name humble themselves and pray and seek My face and turn from their wicked ways, then I will hear from heaven, will forgive their sin and will heal their land.

May I note that with few exceptions, Christians in America who love to quote this verse have never humbled themselves, or sought Gods Face, or turned from their wicked ways...

Then it is followed by a passage in which God makes an acceptance speech:

15 Now My eyes will be open and My ears attentive to the prayer offered in this place. 16 For now I have chosen and consecrated this house that My name may be there forever, and My eyes and My heart will be there perpetually. 17 As for you, if you walk before Me as your father David walked, even to do according to all that I have commanded you, and will keep My statutes and My ordinances, 18 then I will establish your royal throne as I covenanted with your father David, saying, 'You shall not lack a man to be ruler in Israel.' (NASB)

The American Christian loves this kind of passage... They underline all the *"Forevers"*, and the *"Nevers"*, and never even see the "If."

How many times have I been emphatically reminded that God said FOREVER, when the passage starts with the awesome little word "**IF**"?

Go back in this short passage and note first, the words like "forever" and "perpetually" and then go back and carefully read the "**IF**" clause...

***Next comes the part that no modern preacher in his right mind
would ever read from the pulpit or preach on:***

19 "But if you turn away and forsake My statutes and My
commandments which I have set before you, and go and serve other
gods and worship them, 20 then I will uproot you from My land which
I have given you, and this house which I have consecrated for My name
I will cast out of My sight and I will make it a proverb and a byword
among all peoples. 21 As for this house, which was exalted, everyone
who passes by it will be astonished and say, 'Why has the Lord done
thus to this land and to this house?' 22 And they will say, 'Because they
forsook the Lord, the God of their fathers who brought them from the
land of Egypt, and they adopted other gods and worshiped them and
served them; therefore He has brought all this adversity on them.'"
(NASB)

I would be remiss if I failed to mention that Israel, like America,
chose the curse and not the blessing. If you would like to understand
what will soon befall America, you have only to look at what happened
to Israel when they committed the same sins.

Israel had become so evil that when Jeremiah tried to pray for them,
God said:

'Then the Lord said to me, "Even though Moses and Samuel were to
stand before Me, My heart would not be with this people; send them
away from My presence and let them go! 2 And it shall be that when
they say to you, 'Where should we go?' then you are to tell them, 'Thus
says the Lord:

"Those destined for death, to death;
And those destined for the sword, to the sword;
And those destined for famine, to famine;

And those destined for captivity, to captivity."' Jeremiah 15:1 (NASB)

Then, on or about the 10th of Av, 587 BC, Jeremiah walked the Streets of Jerusalem.

In Lamentations chapter 2, we read:

20 See, O Lord, and look!
With whom have You dealt thus?
Should women eat their offspring,
The little ones who were born healthy?
Should priest and prophet be slain
In the sanctuary of the Lord?
21 On the ground in the streets
Lie young and old;
My virgins and my young men
Have fallen by the sword.
You have slain them in the day of Your anger,
You have slaughtered, not sparing.
22 You called as in the day of an appointed feast
My terrors on every side;
And there was no one who escaped or survived
In the day of the Lord's anger.
Those whom I bore and reared,
My enemy annihilated them. (NASB)

Then the Prophet looks at the survivors and cries:

13 How shall I admonish you?
To what shall I compare you,
O daughter of Jerusalem?
To what shall I liken you as I comfort you,
O virgin daughter of Zion?
For your ruin is as vast as the sea;

Who can heal you?
14 Your prophets have seen for you
False and foolish visions;
And they have not exposed your iniquity
So as to restore you from captivity,
But they have seen for you false and misleading oracles.
15 All who pass along the way
Clap their hands in derision at you;
They hiss and shake their heads
At the daughter of Jerusalem,
"Is this the city of which they said,
'The perfection of beauty,
A joy to all the earth'?" (NASB)

Did you get that?

14 Your prophets have seen for you
False and foolish visions;
And they have not exposed your iniquity
So as to restore you from captivity,
But they have seen for you false and misleading oracles. (NASB)

This is the America of today. This next Sunday, all across America, Pastors will look out on their congregations and assure their flocks that God is in control and everything is going to work out well...

Yes, God is in control and He will fulfill his Word!

He will send
"Those destined for death, to death;

And those destined for the sword, to the sword;
And those destined for famine, to famine;
And those destined for captivity, to captivity."'
Should women eat their offspring,
The little ones who were born healthy?

America, like Israel before her, has earned the curse and worked towards her own destruction. When the Republic dies, a New World Order will arise.

✳✳✳

PAGAN RELIGION

The enemy we face today is not atheistic, the enemy is extremely religious.

It is very important to understand the basics of pagan religion. What is happening in the world today is not random but religious. The New World Order is being birthed with religious pageantry. The United States is being brought down with religious fervor. Everything from CERN, to politics, is driven by pagan religion. It is the religion of Nimrod and Babylon, in all its mutated forms, that is the center around which all current events revolve.

"There is a religious institution whose members are the most devout and serious of any faith on earth. Those who are a part of this institution unquestionably believe in a god that directs their activities and they look to this deity with the ultimate hope of gaining his favor. They, unlike many of the people ascribed to the popular religions of today, have no doubt that their god lives and interacts with them. They see the favor their god bestows upon them. The riches and power gained through their piety actively demonstrates the reality of their god's existence. The precepts of their secretive religion are contra to that of the Judeo-Christian religion that values above all, love for their fellow man. They consider the people outside of their group inferior creatures, unworthy of their god, but necessary for manipulation towards the completion of their final objective. Through devotion, submission to the will of their god, and dedication to his secretive plan, they believe that they will

achieve immortality and live in a coming golden age where their god
will appear on earth and rule them in a new paradise of his design."[5]

The "Gospel" of the Illuminati is the ancient GNOSTIC Mysticism.
The real Gospel is Good News... the Gnostic story, not so much.

"Just as Adam and Eve are regarded as central characters in the
Christian creation myth, they are equally as important in that of the
Gnostics. As mentioned in previous articles, the creation of the world
according to Gnostic tradition is an account of the world created not by
the True God, but by a false god. As Adam and Eve were created and
placed in the Garden of Eden in Genesis, the same has been done in
Gnostic scripture:

"However, the demiurge is responsible for the placement of Adam
and Eve in the Garden of Eden. The demiurge has created the fleshly
bodies to entrap the spirits of Adam and Eve. Adam is placed under a
spell of ignorance and put to sleep by the false god. Eve is placed next
to him, and she commands Adam to awaken. When Adam sees Eve, he
believes that she is his creator.

"The demiurge wanted to keep Adam and Eve ignorant; forever
worshiping him. The Gnostics believe that the demiurge was posing as
the false god, thus keeping Adam and Eve under his spell of ignorance.
As long as Adam and Eve believed that he was the only god, they would
worship him forever.

"The serpent is regarded as an evil figure in traditional Christian
stories, but to the Gnostics, the serpent is the hero! The Gnostic text
teaches that as the demiurge tells Adam and Eve that they may help
themselves to anything in the Garden, they are to stay away from the
Tree of Knowledge. As Adam and Eve listen to the serpent, their eyes
are opened, and the spell of ignorance is broken forever. Because they

---

[5] Flynn, Mark A. *Forbidden Secrets of the Labyrinth: the Awakened Ones, the Hidden*
Destiny of America, and the Day after Tomorrow. Defender, 2014.

chose to listen to the serpent, Adam and Eve no longer worship the demiurge, but recognize that there is the True God, and he was not the creator of the evil, imperfect, material world.

"Adam and Eve gave birth to two children, Seth and Norea. The descendants of Seth regard themselves as Sethians, those that have been blessed with the gnosis."[6]

Eve, according to the satanic version, became a completely new creature after she ate the fruit of the Tree of the Knowledge of Good and Evil. Because she recreated herself by an act of her own will, she is seen as virgin born. All ancient goddesses and the Catholic, Mary the Mother of God, are virgin born. Each represent the self-created Eve. In the story there is always a serpent god who represents Lucifer, unfairly judged and punished... once beautiful, now damaged goods. Always in the story there is always a bull or a cow god who represents Jehovah. The serpent god, in every ancient pagan religion, kills the bull or the cow. Adam is strangely missing except as represented in the common man. The unholy trinity is a self-created goddess, a serpent god and a bull... all of mythology, renaming the characters a thousand times, always revolves around these three.

The symbolism is everywhere. The Mary of Catholicism is highly esteemed by Muslims, mentioned in the Koran thirty-three times and the *only* woman mentioned in the Koran, is the pagan representation of the self-created (virgin born) Eve in her fallen state. She was known as Isis who impregnated herself with a prosthetic phallus that she herself made for her brother/husband Osiris, giving birth to the god Horus. She was worshiped in ancient days as the Queen of Heaven and the Mother of God. She is mentioned in Jeremiah 44.

---

[6] *The Gnostic Jesus - Adam and Eve*, www.gnostic-jesus.com/gnostic-jesus/Overview/adam-and-eve.html.

Look at a bullfight in Spain or Mexico. The brightly clothed Matador (killer) represents Lucifer. The bull represents the much larger, bully God who tried to keep Adam and Eve as ignorant slaves and unfairly judged Lucifer. The much smaller Lucifer is smarter and more cunning, and through superior knowledge, kills the bull. The snake always wins in the end.

All the ancient pagan religions, and the Gnostic, or secret knowledge of the secret societies, including Freemasonry, hold that Apollo/Nimrod is going to return and rule the earth in a New World Order. Scripture supports that idea and the idea that the Nephilim return. *Something supernatural is about to happen.* This is the religion of the Illuminati.

Did you know that this is the Gnostic, secret knowledge of the Master Mason? This is the belief system that led Joseph Smith to become founder of the Mormon Church and this is the religious system behind Jehovah's Witnesses. This is the foundation behind the Satanist churches and most major cults. This is the base doctrine of the Church of Rome and the founding belief behind Islam. This teaching drove the first organized religion in Sumer, it is the foundation of Egyptian, Greek and Roman religious cults. This is the central foundation to all pagan religions.

Masons below the thirtieth degree do not know this. The leadership in the Mormon Church, the College of Cardinals, and the Pope, certainly understand, but your average Parish Priest hasn't got a clue. Those in the Watchtower group in New York are fully aware but your average Jehovah's Witnesses have no idea. This is a religion of the elite. This is knowledge reserved for the few; the select. Each of these groups are preparing the common man for the coming of a glorious New World Order... led by a supernatural, messianic figure.

In these last days, Israel's Kabalistic Rabbis are speaking of two Mashiachs: *Mashiach Ben Yosef* and *Mashiach Ben David*. Having never been able to reconcile the prophecies of a conquering Messiah with the prophecies of a suffering and dying Messiah, they have declared that there will be two messiahs, Ben David, the conquering Messiah and Ben Yosef, the suffering and dying Messiah. Of course, it would be difficult to reject the Gospel of Jesus Christ if they were to accept that one individual could fulfill both roles.

The prophetic Rabbis believe that both Messiahs are human and that having fulfilled their roles, they will die as all men die. They say that Mashiach Ben Yosef will die in the Battle with Magog but Mashiach Ben David will show up, kill the bad guys and raise Ben Yosef from the dead. Ben David will then go on to purify Jerusalem and Israel, rebuilding the Temple and restoring the sacrifice.

The strange thing is how closely this follows Christian eschatology which speaks of an Antichrist who dies and a False Prophet who raises him from the dead. One of the heads of the "Beast" has a fatal wound" which is healed. When the people see it, they will marvel.

"One of his heads appeared to be fatally wounded, but his fatal wound was healed. The whole earth was amazed and followed the beast." Revelation 13:3

Those who believe in the Gnostic Gospel are, through demonic works of witchcraft, bribery and blackmail, pulling the strings on every one of the puppets you think are politicians… both the "good" and the "evil". These are the people who remind Donald Trump, every day, that while he is the President, he is one step away from Leavenworth and they have the power to move him there. They will approach whoever is the next president, Republican or Democrat with the same kind of deal. These are the people who whisper in the ear of every Senator and Congressman, on both sides of the aisle, promise to make them very wealthy if they vote as they are told or to kill their children if they should choose to vote wrongly.

Yet Christians, in total ignorance and against all American history, continue to hope that if they can just elect the right person, everything will change…

Let me be blunt. It does not matter who gets in the White House. If we should get a total rebel in the White House, a man who will stand up to them, they will deal with him exactly the way they dealt with Jack Kennedy.

Two things are in operation here:

First, Lucifer, and his demons are determined to undo Babel and return the world to a single government, religion and currency, with Lucifer as god. Your Bible is very clear that he succeeds… for a time.

Second, the United States of America is a major obstacle in their path. The good old USA must crash and burn before the New World Order can rise.

Since God has told us that the New World Order will arise, and since God has very clearly given signs that tell us that this event is imminent, it seems foolish, to me, for a Christian to spend time and effort campaigning for a particular candidate in the hopes that he will stand against Lucifer and thwart that which God himself has told us will happen.

It would seem to me that a Christian's time and energy would be better spent campaigning for Jesus, rescuing souls from Hell and praying that God will protect them and their loved ones from the holocaust that is coming…

I cannot teach you all about pagan religion in this book. You will need to do a lot of homework. I am going to try to give you some of the basics and use these basics to explain current events and point you in the right direction.

Paul stood up in the public square in Athens and said:

"Men of Athens! I see that you are extremely religious in every respect. For as I was passing through and observing the objects of your worship, I even found an altar on which was inscribed: 'TO AN UNKNOWN GOD'…" (Acts 17:22,23)

Paul took the time to study their beliefs, and then, used their own beliefs and words as a foundation from which to present the Gospel in terms to which the Athenians could relate.

Paul would also write:

"I have done this so that we may not be taken advantage of by Satan. For we are not ignorant of his schemes." (2 Corinthians 2:11)

The point here is that you need to understand the religion of the pagan, if you would witness to him you must be aware of Luciferian religion (schemes) so you will not be taken advantage of.

Basics:

- The "gods" are Lucifer himself, fallen angels, Nephilim (offspring of fallen angels and human women) and Gibborum, the offspring of the Nephilim. These are all unredeemable and their spirits roam the earth, possess fallen men and women, or in some cases, are locked up in Hades or the pit.
- The gods who are locked up will escape.
- Antichrist will be the spirit of Nimrod /Apollo/ Apollyon / Abaddon, incarnate in the body of a human leader who has been killed and "resurrected." The man's spirit will be in

Hell, but his body animated and indwelt by the one who is "of the seven" but the eighth.

Pagans believe that the gods are like monkeys; they respond to what they see on earth and do likewise in the heavens. Pagans hold orgies in the spring, believing that the gods will see, get turned on, and that the semen of the gods will inseminate the crops and cause them to grow.

The Luciferians are putting on a massive puppet show, inducing labor pains on the earth, in the sincere belief that the gods will see, respond, and give birth to Apollo who will undo the chaos of Babel, reunite the world, and restore a paradise where they can rule and reign with him forever.

BLUE BLOOD

What does Moses have to do with Rothschild? I am glad you asked...

I believe in the supernatural. I am convinced there were giants on the earth before the flood. I also believe that while they are no longer giants, a race of people has remained on earth who still has the remnants of the DNA of the Sons of God. These people are the elite and the super wealthy of the world.

There once was a strange habit among the European Royalty. Every Monarch in Europe had a *Court Jew*[7]. It was mandatory. This requirement, this habit, descended from the ancient time of Daniel, who was a wise, Jewish advisor to the King of Babylon. Every King had to have a Jew to advise him on important decisions. This practice has followed through every civilized nation since ancient Babylon. These Court Jews became wealthy and powerful.

Mayer Amschel Rothschild (1744-1812) was a Jew. Mayor Rothschild was a *Court Jew* who used his power to amass an untold fortune.

---

[7] "Encyclopedia Judaica." *Suleyman*, www.jewishvirtuallibrary.org/court-jews.

EVIL HIERACHY

Satan or the Devil:
Satan was the covering Angel. He was the one who rebelled against the Most-High God; his own Creator. He was the one who caused a third of the Angels of Heaven to fall with him. He is the one who tempted Eve and caused Adam to sin. He is the one to whom Adam bowed and the one to whom Adam ceded his position of God of this World. He is the father of all that is evil and the chief bad guy of the universe.

Lucifer:
Satan appearing as an Angel of Light. The Devil often plays games, appearing to oppose himself. He will destroy as "Satan" and then appear to rescue as "Lucifer." Lucifer is not opposed to calling himself Jesus and many Christians have fallen when they mistook the Light of Lucifer for the Glory of God.

Fallen Angels:
These are those who fell with Lucifer. These are the principalities and powers. The Prince of Persia who held up the Angel sent to Daniel is among them. These are the spiritual rulers of nations and ethnos.

Osiris:
Also known as Abaddon or Apollyon; Ancient religions tell us that he is the son of Satan and a Nephilim woman. As such, he is two thirds angel and one third man. He is Satan's Seed in a way that mimics Jesus Christ as the Son of God. He is the one "who was, is not, and is to come." (Revelation 17:8) As Apollyon, he is the "*Angel of the Pit*" and the chief demon. It is Osiris who ruled Babylon and built the tower. It is Osiris, who, as the "*Seed of Satan,*" bruised the heel of the Messiah. It is this

Apollyon, who will be released from the pit, torment men, and be incarnated in the body of the Antichrist.

Demons:

Demons are the spirits of the Nephilim. They are neither man nor angel. They are lost and unredeemable. They will be released into the dimension of man, along with Apollyon, in the last day. These are the blood-thirsty ones. Being without bodies, they have no blood. Life is in the blood and it is the blood of human innocents which gives them power. In Babylon, babies were thrown into the fire and sacrificed to demon gods. Today, sacrifice still happens, but it is too rare to provide the power these demons need. Abortion has filled the gap. The blood of a hundred million babies, sacrificed on the altar of abortion, has, in these last days, given incredible power to the demons.

This is how Trump was made President of the United States, how Europe and the United States will fall, and how the New World Order will be born… *all on the blood of innocents*.

The Illuminati:

Thirteen demonized families with the highest concentration of Nephilim tainted DNA on earth. Those at the center of the families buy and sell nations, start wars, loan money, and sell arms to both sides and constantly amass and centralize wealth. These are the rulers of the New World Order.

Blood lines of the Illuminati:[8]

1. The Astor Bloodline

2. The Bundy Bloodline

3. The Collins Bloodline

---

[8] Banerji, Rishabh. "These Are The 13 Families In The World That Apparently Control Everything." *Indiatimes.com*, India Times, 9 Mar. 2018, www.indiatimes.com/culture/who-we-are/these-are-the-13-families-in-the-world-that-apparently-control-everything-from-politics-to-terrorism-257642.html.

4. The DuPont Bloodline

5. The Freeman Bloodline

6. The Kennedy Bloodline

7. The Li Bloodline

8. The Onassis Bloodline

9. The Rockefeller Bloodline

10. The Russell Bloodline

11. The Van Duyn Bloodline

12. The Merovingian Bloodline

13. *The Rothschild Bloodline*

The Outer Family:

Related by blood to the families of the Illuminati, these are not of pure blood, but are related. These are the kings, queens, presidents, dictators and prime ministers of the Caucasian nations. Europe, the Caucasus, England, Russia, the United States and others... these are demonized people; servants of Lucifer and his father. They are, for the most part, puppets of the Luciferian Elite who pull their strings.

Secondary Puppets:

These are the leaders of third world nations. They are not white Caucasians. They have no power beyond that which is granted them by the leaders of the outer family.

It would be good to note here that each ethnic group has its own distinct strengths and weaknesses. I heard a black preacher enumerating the weaknesses of the African Race. He said things that I would be stoned for saying. I am white. Please allow me to say that the weaknesses of the Caucasian race are both different from and perhaps greater than those of other races. White Caucasians are so vain that we painted a Jewish man named Jesus and made him look like us. We want to rule everything, control everything, and own everything and everyone. We were the perfect target for Satan in his bid to unify the world under himself. Some of the most wicked and demonic people on earth are white.

This hierarchy descends to the level of the local Masonic Temple, the Mosques, and the demonized gangs in a Barrio near you. It goes down to the Mason sitting on your local church board. At every level, demons of all ranks inspire and empower those who will do evil.

That is why, the weapons of our warfare must be, *"not of this world,"* but mighty to the bringing down of strongholds.

Rothschild wrote of his personal efforts to strengthen his family bloodline. All of his sons married first cousins and sixteen of the eighteen marriages of his grandchildren were between first cousins.

The Rothschilds, and their extended family, now several hundred years later, hold controlling interest in the Central Banks in all but two nations in the world. They control the Federal Reserve in Washington DC and its counterparts in Beijing, and Moscow. You cannot find an international banker or a CEO of a major international company who is not related to these thirteen families. The presidents of every Ivy League University in the world are related to these families. These families rule the world.

Seven of the thirteen bloodlines of the Illuminati may be traced back to Mayer Amschel Rothschild The Rothchild fortune now controls the world.

The Rothschilds are the undisputed leaders of world government. But we must go back to the family of Moses, the Bible hero, and receiver of the Law.

It is here that the truth will offend the would-be Jews among us... this I cannot avoid.

So, what does Moses have to do with Rothschild? I am glad you asked.

"They waged war against Midian, as the Lord had commanded Moses, and killed every male. 8 Along with the others slain by them, they killed the Midianite kings—Evi, Rekem, Zur, Hur, and Reba, the five kings of Midian. They also killed Balaam son of Beor with the sword. 9 The Israelites took the Midianite women and their children captive, and they plundered all their cattle, flocks, and property. 10 Then they burned all the cities where the Midianites lived, as well as all their encampments, 11 and took away all the spoils of war and the captives, both man and beast. 12 They brought the prisoners, animals, and spoils of war to Moses, Eleazar the priest, and the Israelite community at the camp on the plains of Moab by the Jordan across from Jericho.

13 Moses, Eleazar the priest, and all the leaders of the community, went to meet them outside the camp. 14 But Moses became furious with the officers, the commanders of thousands and commanders of hundreds, who were returning from the military campaign. 15 "Have you let every female live?" he asked them. 16 "Yet they are the ones who, at Balaam's advice, incited the Israelites to unfaithfulness against the Lord in the Peor incident, so that the plague came against the Lord's

community. 17 So now, kill all the male children and kill every woman who has had sexual relations with a man, 18 but keep alive for yourselves all the young females who have not had sexual relations." Numbers 31: 7 NASB

Zipporah, the wife of Moses, was a Midianite (although Numbers 12:1 calls her "a Cushite woman.") More than the incident at Peor, the Midianites, as were the other tribes in the land, of mixed blood, intermarried with the sons of the Nephilim and the Gibborum.

There were giants among the people of Midian. Cush was the eldest son of Ham and Kush is a Hebrew word for African.

God ordered the Israelites to kill *every* man woman and child in the tribe of Midian. Why?

This was not cruel. They carried the deadly strain of hybrid DNA which threatened to pervert the bloodline of Abraham and prevent the birth of the Messiah. Saving the virgin girls alive most likely lead to the unholy mixing of DNA. God destroyed the tribes living in the Promised Land for the *same reason* He had sent the Flood.

Moses was already married to a Midianite, and many, including myself, believe that it is the children of Moses and Zipporah whose blood now flows throw the veins of the Rothschilds and their extended family.

Jesus spoke often of separating the tares from the wheat, the chaff from the grain and other illustrations of a final, earthly, separation. The church has taken this as separating the saved from the unsaved, but Jesus was speaking to Jews. It is within the realm of possibility that Jesus was talking about separating all of mankind; removing the unredeemable, those with the deadly DNA. (I would note here that the separation of the tares and the wheat, unlike the Pre-Trib story, has the tares removed *first*.)

Is it possible there are two races of men dwelling together on this planet? Could one be a mixed and perverted race, blood relatives of the fallen angels who rule the world, in the name of Lucifer?

AMERICA AS BABYLON

Rebuilding the Tower

America's connection to Babylon is almost as old as her connection to Israel. The connection dates to the earliest days of the first colonies. It was not long after the first colonies rose out of the American wilderness that the Vatican, and especially the Society of Jesus, began to see the potential of the New World. There was business to be done and wealth to be gained. Certainly, the Catholic Church must have a hand in its growth!

The Catholic Church, they were certain, should rule the world, but there was a problem on the new continent: America was peopled by those who had been persecuted by the Catholic Church. America was Protestant to the core. A Catholic priest would have been like a fish out of water in the Colonies! The question arose, "How does the Church of Rome control a distinctly anticatholic, protestant people and their land?"

The Roman Church, by combining the best of paganism with the outward form and the vocabulary of Christianity, had become Lucifer's latest great hope for bringing in the New World Order that would unite mankind under a single government, with a single flag and a single language. The Pope would serve as the new messiah and king of the Kingdom with the Vatican as capital and Latin as its language... This had been the plan from before Lucifer ever visited with Constantine, giving him a dream and a flag.

The Inquisition was going well in most of the world, including South America, but North America was a problem. The answer was to be found in secret societies.

There was a secret society known as The Knights Templar. Early in the twelfth century, nine knights took a vow to protect pilgrims traveling through the Holy Land. More knights joined the cause and the organization grew. They gained fame, power, and wealth, as their influence spread.

Another secret society were the Rosicrucians. Said to have been founded by Christian Rosenkranz in the 15th century, this society is regarded as one of the oldest societies. The Rosicrucian's ultimate objective as a group is the "universal reformation of mankind." To them, this meant turning the world to occultism. The Rosicrucian's official symbol is a rose on a cross.

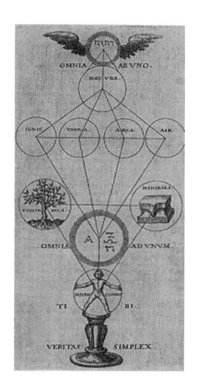

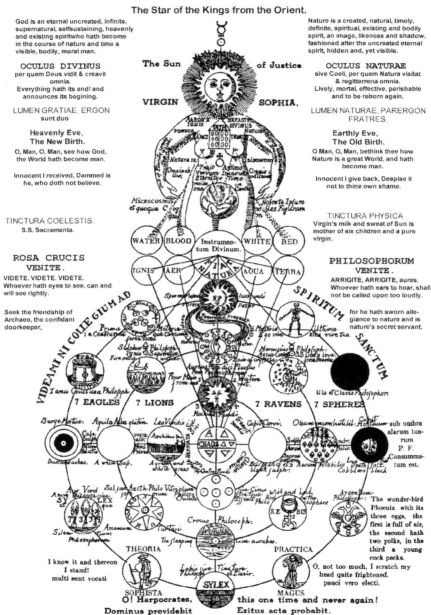

The Heavenly and Earthly Eve, Mother of all Creatures in Heaven and on Earth.

The Star of the Kings from the Orient.

With the Rosicrucians, being openly occultic, and any of The Knights Templar still surviving being super consecrated Catholics, neither group was likely to make inroad into North American society. What was needed was a *new* "Protestant" secret society. It would be the Jesuits who would start an organization for the Protestants and make certain that the Pope himself would forbid Catholics to join the group.

The first Grand Masonic Lodge was founded in 1717 in London, England, the nation from which most immigrants were arriving in America. The British had a "Christian" heritage and culture. What better way to slip in to America than to arrive using "Christian" language?

Since the secret nature of the Masons has allowed them to paint a very different public portrait of themselves than truth would permit, I must begin by using one of their most famous members, to introduce them, Albert Pike:

Every Masonic Lodge is a Temple of religion; and its teachings are instructions in religion. (Morals and Dogma page 213)

All truly dogmatic religions have issued from the Kabbalah and return to it: everything scientific and grand in the religious dreams of all the Illuminati... is borrowed from the Kabbalah; all the Masonic associations owe to it their Secrets and their Symbols. (Morals and Dogma, pg 744,)

Masonry, like all the religions, all Mysteries, Hermeticism, and Alchemy, conceals its secrets from all except the Adepts and Sages, or the Elect, and uses false explanations and misinterpretations of its symbols to mislead those who deserve to be mislead... So Masonry jealously conceals its secrets, and intentionally leads conceited interpreters astray. (Morals and Dogma Pages 104-105) Albert Pike[9]

---

[9] [Pike, Albert]. *Morals and Dogma of the Ancient and Accepted Scottish Rite of Freemasonry: Prepared for the Supreme Council of the Thirty-Third Degree for the Southern Jurisdiction of the United States and Published by Its Authority.: Esoteric Book, for Scottish Rite Use Only; to Be Returned upon Withdrawal of Death of Recipient. 1950.*

It is interesting that in Hebrew, there is no word for Babylon, only *Babel*. Nebuchadnezzar was the King of Babel, the King of Confusion.

"God is not the author of confusion, but of peace, as in all churches of the saints." 1 Corinthians 14:33 (NASB) This scripture is true, but it is limited to inside the churches of the Saints. The word Babel means confusion or disorder. Outside the church, in the world, God is the creator and author of confusion. He did it at Babel.

Before the confusion, God's testimony concerning mankind was, *"nothing which they purpose to do will be impossible for them."* God's answer to this threat was confusion, *Babel*.

I am convinced that next to the Cross of Christ, Babel was the largest single blow ever dealt to Lucifer and his cause. Separated into tongues, tribes, and nations, by the hand of God, mankind was no longer able to accomplish anything. Man became extremely limited by this division and they still are.

There have been a long string of attempts by Lucifer to undo Babel. The first was Egypt, followed by Greece, Rome, Germany, Great Britain and many others. It is an interesting journey to travel through history and to trace the journey from kingdom to kingdom but that is beyond the scope of this book.

Having mentioned Egypt, I will mention that under Greece, most of the world was briefly united with a common language and under Rome, that same group was united through military force.

That power, while perhaps shared in a small part by Russia and China, is the property of the United States of America. Representative Ron Paul of Texas told that the United States, as a nation, has military bases in more than 130 nations.[10] No country on earth comes even close

---

[10] "Ron Paul Says U.S. Has Military Personnel in 130 Nations and 900 Overseas Bases." *@Politifact*, www.politifact.com/truth-o-

to this number. the United States is the undisputed champion of the world. In political clout, military force, commerce, and in a multitude of other areas.

This is just a small part of America's story. America's story goes back to ancient Egypt.

Bear with me through a bit of Egyptian folklore…

There is a story about a weird little family of gods. These gods existed, but the stories that surround them have been greatly exaggerated. It is a perverted story about Osiris, Set, (not Seth) and Isis, who were brother and sister gods.

Osiris and Isis, brother and sister, fell in love and married. They were both brother and sister and then husband and wife. Before they could have sex and make a little baby god, the evil brother Set, became jealous and killed Osiris. He cut Osiris into fourteen pieces and spread his parts all over Egypt.

Isis was distraught. Still a virgin, she had no heir. Desperate, she set out across Egypt and gathered up all the parts of her brother/husband and found all except one. His penis was missing. It had been thrown in the Nile and had been eaten by a fish.

Isis sewed together all thirteen of the parts she had found. Osiris, of course, was still dead but at least he looked like himself. Nonetheless, he had no penis and could not make a baby for her. Not to be undone, Isis made a magic dildo, attached it as if it were his penis, and impregnated herself.

Isis gave birth to a baby boy whom she named Horus. Horus was, according to Isis, the reincarnation of her brother/husband Osiris. Thus, he was her son, her brother, and her husband. Then, when Horus was just twelve years old, Isis married him and took him to her bed.

---

meter/statements/2011/sep/14/ron-paul/ron-paul-says-us-has-military-personnel-130-nation/.

Being the Chief Goddess *and* the Wife of the Chief God, Isis became the Queen of Heaven when her life on earth was done. Horus was both god and the son of god. This is how Isis became the Virgin Mother of God, a title she retains today, although she has been baptized as Mary, Queen of Heaven and Mother of God.

All the pieces of the story Lucifer overheard in Heaven were accomplished, albeit in a perverted and twisted manner.

"The children gather wood, and the fathers kindle the fire, and the women knead dough to make cakes for the queen of heaven; and they pour out drink offerings to other gods in order to spite Me." Jeremiah 7:18
(God)

Isis

Osiris

Thirteen into one is what you need to notice in this story. The Egyptians took the story of Nimrod, gave him an Egyptian name, embellished the details, and gave it a distinctly Egyptian twist. There are extrabiblical stories of Nimrod, that speak of his wife, Semiramis, who outlived him, married their son, and continued as Queen in Babylon long after his death. This connects him to the Egyptian account of Osiris.

As Scripture so clearly points out in the story of Moses, the Egyptian Magicians were a powerful group of people. Although God won, it should be pointed out turning sticks into snakes on demand is a talent envied by modern magicians. Keep in mind, they had no time to prepare a stunt. Until Aaron threw down his staff, they had no idea what was going to happen.

Exodus 7:11 Pharaoh then summoned wise men and sorcerers, and the Egyptian magicians also did the same things by their secret arts: 12

Each one threw down his staff and it became a snake. But Aaron's staff swallowed up their staffs.

***

EGYPTIAN MAGIC

Egyptian magic forms the base of *all* magic. Egyptians inherited magic from Babylon. It was in Egypt where the Occultic Arts were perfected. All occultism and all magic can be traced directly back to Egypt.

Modern Masons are captivated by Greek and Roman architecture. They love the stories of Hiram Abiff, the imaginary architect of Solomon's Temple, but it is Egyptian magic and Egyptian Myths that capture the Masons' imaginations.

1 Kings 5:1 When Hiram king of Tyre heard that Solomon had been anointed king to succeed his father David, he sent his envoys to Solomon, because he had always been on friendly terms with David. 2 Solomon sent back this message to Hiram... NIV

Albert Pike was a powerful warlock and magician. In his greatly revered Masonic Textbook, *Morals and Dogma*, Pike writes the following:

We have therefore, in the 24th degree (Masonic Ritual), recited the principal incidents in the legend of Osiris and Isis ... Everything good in Nature comes from Osiris... Osiris was the image of generative power. This was expressed by his symbolic statues ... Osiris and Isis were the Sun and Moon ... and is the All-Seeing Eye in our Lodges ... Osiris was invoked as the God that resides in the Sun (pgs. 474-477)

"The Supreme being of the Egyptians was Amun, a secret and concealed God, the Unknown Father of the Gnostics, the Source of Divine Life, and of all force, the Plenitude of all, comprehending all things in Himself, the original Light. He creates nothing, but everything eminates from Him: and all other Gods are but his manifestations. From Him, by the utterance of a Word, eminated Neith, the Divine Mother of all things, the Primitive THOUGHT, the FORCE, that puts everything in movement, the SPIRIT everywhere extended, the Diety of Light and Mother of the Sun. .....Of the Supreme beings, Osiris was the image, Source of all Good in the Moral and Physical World, and a constant foe of Typhone, the Genius of Evil, the Satan of Gnosticism, brute matter, deemed to be always at fued with the spirit that flowed from the Diety; and over whom Har-Oeri, (Horus) the Redeemer, Son of Isis.[11]

There are several versions of the story of Osiris, but for us it is most important to understand that Set cut Osiris into *exactly* fourteen pieces and scattered them around Egypt. Isis then found thirteen parts. She sowed thirteen of his parts back together, but the fourteenth part was replaced and inserted into the thirteen... Did you follow that?

Uniting thirteen parts into a single unit and then adding a fourteenth, distinctly different part into the middle is the most powerful principle of Egyptian, and therefore, Masonic magic.

If you remember your history, in the start of America, thirteen colonies were sewn together to make the United States. Soon a fourteenth, yet separate piece was added. Washington DC was thrown *into the middle*. The <u>most important part</u> but *distinct, different, and set apart.* Washington DC is not a state but, out of Washington, more states can be added. This is the reason the United States could grow into the nation it has become.

Mighty, Egyptian magic, brought by the Masons, formed the nation now called The United States of America.

"But...the United States is (or at least was) a Christian nation! How dare you suggest that the United States was founded on Egyptian magic!"

---

[11].[Pike, Albert]. *Morals and Dogma of the Ancient and Accepted Scottish Rite of Freemasonry: Prepared for the Supreme Council of the Thirty-Third Degree for the Southern Jurisdiction of the United States and Published by Its Authority.: Esoteric Book, for Scottish Rite Use Only; to Be Returned upon Withdrawal of Death of Recipient. 1950.*

PART TWO

The True History of America

AMERICA

Christian People, Pagan Government

The Pilgrims, and many who followed, *were* Christian. By the time the American Government was formed, the United States had been through some ups and downs in the area of religion, but there had been great revival and most Americans were, at least nominally, Christian. There were enough Christians that no one who could not attract the Christian vote, could hope to win any election.

For that reason, the wealthy members of the secret societies, who had immigrated by the droves, joined churches presenting some very pagan ideas in very Christian language. They supported the churches, the seminaries, and paid preachers' salaries. It was *they* who controlled money. No one could argue with these men!

While the people were mostly Christian, it was a group of masonic pagans who drew the plans for our nation. These secret societies presented a very pagan government to a very Christian people, written in a language they could accept.

You will notice, for instance, that the word p*rovidence* is used throughout early government papers of the United States. Even in those days, the word providence was a term used much more by Deists than Christians, but Christian people interpreted it as meaning their God. The Masonic Deists who wrote the word providence were referring to the impersonal Creator whom they believed created everything, invented human government, and stepped back to watch what happened.

The idea of sin and Savior was abhorrent to Masons and Deists, and any idea that God had or would intervene in the affairs of men was completely rejected. However, if the Christians understood the words Providence and God, in the documents, as referring to their God, the plan was working as designed.

I should note that the doctrine of the Deists and the Masons are in sharp contrast, one with the other. The Deists claim a Creator God who never intervenes in human affairs, while the Masons embrace every pagan god in existence. The fact remains, most of the Founding Fathers claimed to be both Deists and Masons. What they actually believed would be difficult to determine.

We will speak of the Founding Fathers in a later chapter, but here it is enough to declare my belief that few, if any of them made it to Heaven.

In the strongest of the Egyptian magic and ceremony, *thirteen are sewn together as one, and then a fourteenth is inserted into the middle.* With Egyptian magic, a stone, *Phallus of Osiris*, is raised in every place. In the Greek architecture which developed out of that magic, *a dome always represents the womb of Isis.* A Phallus overlooks the womb of Isis. An Osirian Penis shoots 555 feet (6,660 inches) into the sky.

The Capital Dome is located in the middle of Washington DC. The Washington Monument located in the center of that same city measuring precisely and exactly 6,660 inches or 555 feet tall, standing straight up, overlooking the Capital Dome.

It was God Almighty who divided mankind into tribes and tongues and nations. How then did the Luciferians, who were working with the Devil to undo Babel, convince *Christians* that uniting people from every tribe, tongue and nation, under one flag, with one language and one culture, was a God thing?

More than that, how did we ever accept a 6,660 inch tall representation of the phallus of Osiris as a fitting monument to a "Christian" President?

The government of the United States was founded by Luciferians. These men followed a plan, developed in Hell and revealed to men like Sir Francis Bacon and Adam Weishaupt. Everything from thirteen colonies being united into one to the choice of the year 1776 was based on Egyptian religion, taught by Weishaupt and written by Sir Francis, in a book called, "The New Atlantis." All this was done in secret and Christians were taught that these were "Christian" principles.

The United States was formed by a violent revolution. It could have been founded without war or bloodshed, but it could not be simply "founded;" It had to be *birthed*. Birth produces a living thing, and the United States had to live as a spiritual entity. Birth cannot be accomplished without blood and pain. There had to be *pain and bloodshed*; thus, the Revolution.

The phoenix dies in the fire and is birthed, born anew, out of the smoke and flames of its mother. The United States is, to the pagans, the mother of the New World Order. What was accomplished on one continent must now be repeated on a world-wide scale. Like a phoenix born out of the fire and smoke of its mother; born stronger, better, and bigger, than its predecessor the New World Order will rise out of the ashes of the United States,

Birth involves pain and blood. The phoenix is born out of the fire and smoke of its predecessor... *These are basic truths in the Luciferian and Masonic religions.* Remember that the gods are inspired to act and controlled by that which happens on earth. They are *imitators*. The Luciferians, whether they be the Elite who understand and commune with Lucifer, or the Roman Jesuit, or the Muslim Cleric, or the American Politician, all understand that the new cannot be birthed without pain, death, bloodshed, and fire. (This is why Sherman had to burn the South and the Twin Towers had to fall.)

The Luciferians are committed to the idea of a New World Order:

- They believe that Apollo will rise, incarnate, in the body of a man. That cannot happen unless a man dies.
- They see the entire world, under the command of Apollo, healthy, rich, and united... a global version of the United

States. For that to happen, the United States must crash and burn.

- New York City is the greatest city on earth and home to the United Nations. When New York, and the United Nations burn; out of the ashes, like a phoenix, the New World Order will be born.
- When Washington DC burns, a new city will be born. What has been the capital of the United States will be reborn as the capital city of the world.

This birth requires excruciating, bone breaking pain, and extreme bloodshed. This is a reasonable sacrifice in the mind of the Luciferian, the Jesuit, and the Master Mason, all whom consider themselves to be above the fray and immune to the pain.

Everything and everyone around them will die, but they are the elect, and as such, will survive to rule and reign with Apollo in the New World Order.

It takes hundreds of hours of study and the help of God's Holy Spirit to really understand the big picture. Please note that this is the inverse of the picture painted in Scripture. They fit together like a hand in a glove.

Why would Americans want to see America burn? *Now you know.*

Why would Americans encourage rioting and bloodshed? *You have the answer.*

Why would a Caucasian Jew, a billionaire named George Soros, give millions of dollars to Black Lives Matters and Muslim radicals in the United States? *If you understand his religion, you have the answer.*

This is the inverse of the picture painted in Scripture, but they fit together like a hand in a glove.

Why am I sharing this, knowing that it could cost my life and the lives of my family?

"I have done this so that we may not be taken advantage of by Satan. For we are not ignorant of his schemes."

That which God has torn asunder, let no man reassemble.

THE TRINITY OF BABYLON:
ROME, ENGLAND, AND THE UNITED STATES OF AMERICA

What Scripture calls *Babylon* has confused many people.

Is Babylon a city in Iraq? Is it Rome? Is it the Roman Catholic Church? Is it England and the British Throne? Is it an Empire, a nation, or a City?

Books have been written supporting and defending each of these ideas. Social media is filled with arguments from individuals taking various positions. Those who argue one position over the other simply fail to see the big picture. Having become obsessed with one aspect they reject all but their own idea. Because they see absolute truth in a small piece, they assume that anything else, and anything beyond or different from what they have discovered, must be false.

Babylon did not start with the city and empire that conquered Israel and took Daniel captive. Babylon started on the plain of Shinar, at a place known as Sumer. It was from Shinar that Nimrod ruled, and it was in Shinar that the great tower, known as Babel, was built. It was in Sumer that the first pagan religion was codified and imposed on the people. The R*eligion of Sumer* is the Mother of *all* pagan religions in the world.

Apart from genuine, biblical Judaism and Christianity, there is no religion, including Atheistic Humanism, that cannot be traced back to Nimrod, the Plain of Shinar, and Sumer. Every age, and every world empire, has been built on the foundations of Babel. Every age, and every world empire, has modified the outer trappings of the original pagan religion to make it their own.

When Babylon later ruled the world, they changed the names of the gods. They also changed outward signs, symbols and forms of the religion, making it their own.

In succession, each nation modified the religion for themselves.

The Egyptians called Nimrod *Osiris.*
The Greeks called Osiris *Apollo/Horus.*
The Romans called Apollo *Apollyon.*

The Hebrews called Apollo *Abaddon*.

NOTE: All of these names can be traced back to words meaning "Rebel" or "rebellion."

Each kingdom added to the story changing it to fit their own culture and liking, each adding new and strange details to the legend. The Egyptian form of the religion remains the chief form. It is Egyptian Magic that permeates the New World Order and motivates its devotees. At the heart though, nothing changed. The religion of Rome was the religion of Sumer. The fallen angels of Genesis 6 were seen, neither as angels, nor fallen; they were gods and they controlled the destinies of men and nations.

Israel, from the beginning, was a thorn in the side of Osiris. Truth threatens lies, and Jehovah threatened Lucifer.

From the days of Babylon, through Egypt, Greece, and Rome, Judaism was the enemy of men and nations. Every effort was made, in every age, to destroy Israel and its people. Then, during the days of the Roman Empire, Jesus was born, and the Church was birthed.

Where Israel was a nation and seldom carried its ideas beyond her borders, Christianity was an *idea*. Christianity knew no borders and spread like wildfire. The more Christians Rome killed, the more Christians there were. Christianity was taking over the world at an unbelievable pace.

The Roman Emperor, Constantine, woke up to the reality that he was outnumbered. His soldiers would no longer slaughter Christians, his soldiers were becoming Christians! Constantine and the religion of Nimrod were on the way out. Lucifer too, saw the problem and came to Constantine. Appearing as an Angel of Light, Lucifer gave the emperor a dream. Constantine saw a cross and the words written, "In hoc signo vinces," "In this sign, conquer." At that moment, the war against Christ, and the Saints, was forever changed.

Constantine told that in the dream Christ appeared with the heavenly symbol, and told him to make the labarum for his army in that form. The sign was Chi (X) traversed by Rho (P) to give the Chi Rho: ☧, a symbol representing the first two letters of the Greek spelling of the word Christos or Christ.

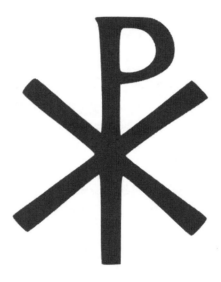

Suddenly, the ancient religion of Sumer was baptized as "Christian."
Every pagan god was given a Christian name:
Osiris became "The Father."
Horus became "The Son"
Isis was baptized "Mary"

Mary became "The Queen of Heaven," and *"The Mother of God,"* titles held by Semiramis, Isis, Tammuz, and a number of other goddesses.

Even the ancient pagan gods became known as *Saint Peter, Saint Thomas, Saint Phillip*, and thousands more…

The Romans made the Altar of Christ into the Altar of Baal.

Fortunately, a bold man by the name of Martin Luther challenged everything the Roman Catholic Church had done. Protestants were birthed and eventually came out of that mess washed in the Blood of the Lamb. and filled with the Spirit. They ran as far as they could run but Rome continued to slaughter true, believers. God however was faithful, and his Church flourished and grew.

Unfortunately, protestants did not run far enough. They continued to view the Roman Church as a church that had fallen into sin… they never saw that the Roman Church had never been Christian and was, at its very core, the religion of Sumer and Babel.

England

England would rule the world next. There was a time when it was said that "The sun never sets on the British Empire." The Jesuits were involved in English government, and God's people fled to America for the freedom of religion. Much could be said about England, but our purpose here is to point out that power passed from Rome, through England, to America. British Royalty were, and are, of demon blood. Every American President, save one, has been related to the British

Crown.[12] The Anglican Church is the bastard daughter of Rome and the religion of Babel passed through England to America.

England became Babylon and the United States, birthed out of England, became the *Daughter of Babylon.*

Remember, 1492 was an earth-shaking year:

- The Jewish community in Spain was the largest in the world.
- Islam was beaten, and Catholicism reigned supreme.
- Father Juan Perez got Columbus in front of the King.
- The Jews were given thirty days to convert or leave Spain.
- The Government confiscated all wealth and property of the Jews.
- The King used the money from the Jews to finance the voyage of Columbus.
- Columbus discovered America.
- America would become the next safe-haven and home for the Jews.

---

[12] Farberov, Snejana. "All Presidents Bar One Are Directly Descended from a Medieval English King." *Daily Mail Online*, Associated Newspapers, 5 Aug. 2012, www.dailymail.co.uk/news/article-2183858/All-presidents-bar-directly-descended-medieval-English-king.html.

America

America would not only become a home to the Jews but Christians from all over Europe, would flee the persecution of the Roman Church and come to America. Soon the area that is now the very pagan North-East in the United States, was home to the largest Evangelical Christian Community in the world and Rome was more than aware of that fact.

Soon, pagan Europeans with money, power and influence, began to flood into America. As in the days of Constantine, this called for stealth and became an undercover operation. Jesuits, who controlled Secret Societies, including the Masons, posed as Protestant ministers and came to America like a flood. These men were not Christian. They wanted to rule an Evangelical and Protestant people for the Pope. Supported by Rome, and with the blessings of Lucifer, these men had both money and power. Soon they would govern the new America.

Using Christian words and phrases, these Jesuits sold demonic ideas to Christians who accepted the noble sounding ideas as if they were Christian ideas, coming from God himself. Since the day the Tower of Babel came down, and the people were scattered, it has been the goal of Lucifer to reunite the world.

This is the goal of the New World Order today and this was the goal of the United States' founding fathers. Working with an idea first proposed by Plato, then developed by a novel, *The New Atlantis*, by Sir Francis Bacon, these non-Christian "Founding Fathers," divided the land into exactly thirteen colonies.

This was not an accident. It was Egyptian magic.

Remember:
Set cut Osiris into fourteen pieces.
Isis found thirteen pieces but one piece, his penis, was lost.

Isis sewed the pieces together, made a fake penis with her own hands and impregnated herself.

The Founding Fathers of the United States divided the new land into thirteen pieces, sewed them together, constructed a penis (called the "Washington Monument,") inserted it into the middle, in a separate district, distinct from the thirteen, called Washington D.C.

They brought people from every nation, tongue and tribe, and united them with a single government, culture and language. This would form the most powerful nation the world had ever known.

Based on history and Scripture:[13]

Rome is Babylon and the Roman System is Babylonian.
Islam is the bastard son of Babylon.
England is the heir of Babylon.
The United States is the Daughter of Babylon.

Babylon is a religion, a system, and a church. Islam is a form of Babylonian Religion as Babylon ruled the world under the Ottoman Empire. We are all connected.

The day is coming…the United States must die, and the United States of the World must be born. All the chaos you see on the news is provoked by these people, for that purpose. America will one day give birth to the New World Order.

Lucifer's quest continues to undo Babel on a worldwide scale. Lucifer plans, as he did at Babel, to crown himself as God.

---

[13] 1 Peter 5:13

The current reigning Babylon is the United States of America. In every way, America rules the world. The wealth, the power, the luxury, the sin, and the perversion of the world, are all centered in America.

The United States is the *Nation of Babylon*,

New York City is the *City of Babylon*.

In New York Harbor stands the *"Whore of Babylon."*.

Islam is the *Bastard son of Babylon*

Rome is the religion, and the power, of Babylon. ... It is one big family and we will all take part in the end and we will all suffer the wrath of God.

Understand that the Hindu gods are the gods of Babel with Indian names.

Mother Earth is a Babylonian god.

Atheistic Humanism is a form of the religion of Babel.

The current Pope, a Jesuit, is trying to regress the entire world and then unite the world under the raw religion of Babel. Catholics, Atheists, Protestants, Hindus, Muslims, Buddhists, African Animists, witches and warlocks... all religions will unite around Isis, "Queen of Heaven" and "Mother of God." Osiris will rule the world until Jesus comes.

FOUNDING FATHERS
And the lies we all believed.

Masonic Christians have, of late, produced some slick books, magazines and videos designed to reassure the comfortable Christian that America really is the Christian nation they so desperately wish it to be.

I was sent a video series by a man who had carefully moved his camera around the Capitol Rotunda and having avoided almost ninety percent of the artwork on the walls and ceilings, carefully, very, very carefully showed us the two or three Christian paintings and a single Christian statue that adorn the room. In the most soothing of terms, he reassured us, that despite anything we might have heard to the contrary, our Capitol was a Christian place, designed and built for us by the most Christian of people. I will never figure out how he kept almost everything in that space either grossly out of focus or out of the frame altogether.

The building is topped by a pagan idol. The inside of the dome is covered by a painting called *The Apotheosis (Deification) of George Washington.* That Painting shows Washington, enthroned in Heaven, surrounded by almost every pagan god known to ancient Greece. The painting itself is surrounded by seventy-two five pointed stars, a design created by those who understood both that seventy-two is the number of the Sons of God among whom God divided the nations of the earth and that in Egyptian magic, that arrangement is said to attract and hold (i.e. prevent the escape of) those Sons of God and others. (This is just the beginning of what is inside this building. If there were 38 degrees in the Masonic Lodge, I would bet that the man who made that "Christian Video" held them all!)

I have heard Christians complaining that we are somehow rewriting history! They make that claim because they have never read any history that was not included in a textbook given them by people who were much more interested in what their students believed than in truth!

Honestly, it does not take a Ph.D. to look through the history books written in the early eighteen-hundreds and compare them with the books printed at the end of the 19th century and the beginning of the 20th century to understand that there was a great revision of history. *The problem is that it was not done to convince us that our forefathers were not Christian but rather that they were.*

Somewhere, probably in the early decades of the 19th century, some of our educators decided that our early leaders should be portrayed, not only as Christians, but almost superhuman. Armed with such a belief, they set out to "Christianize" American history. They were so good at what they did that by the time I was in school, General Custer had done the Christian thing when he killed off all those horrible, ungodly, nasty Indians!

The Apotheosis of Washington

GEORGE WASHINGTON

There is considerable debate on the question of Washington's religion. Some would insist that his use of the word "God" in speeches proves him Christian. He attended church frequently and such attendance proves his faith. Never mind that a Presbyterian Pastor, who knew him, is quoted as saying, "Sir, George Washington was a Deist, not a Christian." Do not even consider that his Presbyterian Pastor in Washington DC wrote, "Washington and his group always stood up and left the building before communion was served," Yet, in the history books our first President was a Christian and every textbook showed him on his knees! Perhaps he was praying to his horse, I do not know. But I do know that a Deist believed that God never answered prayer. As a Mason, he would have believed in Egyptian magic and all the pagan gods. How he and his friends reconciled that is a mystery to me.

Never mind that Washington was a Mason and that he is frequently shown in Masonic uniform in paintings of the era. We have both written transcripts and paintings of the day that Washington, in full Masonic regalia, laid the Cornerstone for the Capitol Building in Washington DC. Yes, Washington was a Master Mason, to whit I reproduce the following correspondence.

"At the Quarterly Communication, held March 5, 1792, the Right Worshipful Grand Master Jonathan B. Smith informed the Mason Brethren that in conformity to the resolve of this Grand Lodge, he had, in company with the Grand Officers and the Rev. Brother Dr. Smith, presented the address to our illustrious Brother *George Washington*, and had received an answer, which was read.

"To the ancient YORK MASONS of the
Jurisdiction of Pennsylvania:

"Gentlemen and Brothers,

"I receive your kind Congratulations
"with the purest sensations of fraternal affection:—and
"from a heart deeply impressed with your generous
"wishes for my present and future happiness, I beg

"you to accept my thanks.

"At the same time I request you will
"be assured of my best wishes and earnest prayers
"for your happiness while you remain in this terres-
"tial Mansion, and that we may thereafter meet
"as brethren in the Eternal Temple of the
"Supreme Architect.
Go. Washington"[14]

---

[14] "Washington's Masonic Correspondence." *Alice's Adventures in Wonderland, by Lewis Carroll,* Project Gutenberg, www.gutenberg.org/files/29949/29949-h/29949-h.htm.

I am theologically and doctrinally convinced that the "*Eternal Temple of the Supreme Architect*" is to be found somewhere in the hindermost part of Sheol, perhaps beneath the Pit.

I encourage you to read up on Deism. (A good book to read is *Six Historic Americans* by John Remsburg, especially Chapter 3.)

THOMAS JEFFERSON

Thomas Jefferson has been portrayed as a Christian man. I could wax eloquently on the man's very unchristian attributes. I shall refrain from doing so for want of brevity.

Let it suffice to point out that the man was so unhappy with Christianity and the Gospel as presented in Scripture that he took it upon himself to cut apart his new Testament, line by line and verse by verse, using a straight razor. He then took a blank journal and, having thrown away all the parts with which he disagreed, proceeded to rearrange the parts that he, in his infinite Christian wisdom decided were inspired, and paste them into that journal. That which remained (about 20%) he called his "Bible." It is now called "Jefferson's Bible"[15] and it may be purchased on line or at most book stores.

Jefferson's Bible
known.

---

[15] Jefferson, Thomas, et al. *The Jefferson Bible: the Life and Morals of Jesus of Nazareth, Extracted Textually from the Gospels in Greek, Latin, French & English.* Smithsonian Books, 2011.

The Egyptian's placed an Obelisk at the entrance of their temples and graves, sometimes more than one, something Jefferson must have known.

Why would Jefferson want to have an Egyptian Obelisk as a gravestone?

Before his death, he wrote and drew his wishes out on a piece of paper:

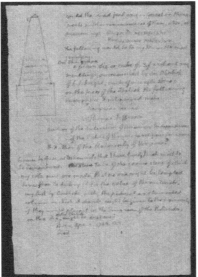

I really do not see any reason to pursue this man further.

BENJAMIN FRANKLIN

May I be so free as to start by noting that it was under Benjamin Franklin's house, having been buried there since his time, that investigators found the burned and mutilated remains of multiple persons. That seems like as good a place as any to start our little biography. During a 1998 renovation of Franklin's London residence, more than 1,200 burned, separated and mutilated human bones were discovered buried in his basement.[16]

Bones in Franklin's Basement

Franklin was associated with secret societies in the United States, London and Paris. While it is useful for our purposes to speak of the

---

[16] Schultz, Colin. "Why Was Benjamin Franklin's Basement Filled With Skeletons?" *Smithsonian.com*, Smithsonian Institution, 3 Oct. 2013, www.smithsonianmag.com/smart-news/why-was-benjamin-franklins-basement-filled-with-skeletons-524521/.

Masons in the US, it is The Hellfire Club[17] in London, (which was actually called the Order of the Friars of St. Francis of Wycombe) that was the most openly evil. They bought an old church and rebuilt it and had a motto from Rabelais reading "Fay ce que voudras" (Do What Thou Wilt) carved over the door. They were famous for wild sex, drunkenness, and occult workings.

I believe that the easiest way to show the man's character would be to reprint his letter to a single, young friend.

June 25, 1745

My dear Friend,

I know of no medicine fit to diminish the violent natural inclinations you mention; and if I did, I think I should not communicate it to you. Marriage is the proper remedy. It is the most natural State of Man, and therefore the State in which you are most likely to find solid happiness. Your reasons against entering into it at present, appear to me not well-founded. The circumstantial advantages you have in view by postponing it, are not only uncertain, but they are small in comparison with that of the thing itself, the being married and settled. It is the man and woman united that make the compleat human being. Separate, she wants his force of body and strength of reason; he, her softness, sensibility and acute discernment. Together they are more likely to succeed in the world. A single man has not nearly the value he would have in that state of union. He is an incomplete animal. He resembles the odd half of a pair of scissors. If you get a prudent healthy wife, your industry in your profession, with her good economy, will be a fortune sufficient.

---

[17] Haden-Guest, Anthony. "How Debauched Was The Hellfire Club?" *The Daily Beast*, The Daily Beast Company, 11 Apr. 2015, www.thedailybeast.com/how-debauched-was-the-hellfire-club.

But if you will not take this counsel, and persist in thinking a commerce with the sex inevitable, then I repeat my former advice, that in all your amours you should prefer old women to young ones. You call this a paradox, and demand my reasons. They are these:

1.. Because as they have more knowledge of the world and their minds are better stor'd with observations, their conversation is more improving and more lastingly aggreable.

2. Because when women cease to be handsome, they study to be good. To maintain their influence over men, they supply the diminution of beauty by an augmentation of utility. They learn to do a 1000 services small and great, and are the most tender and useful of all friends when you are sick. Thus they continue amiable. And hence there is hardly such a thing to be found as an old woman who is not a good woman.

3. Because there is no hazard of children, which irregularly produc'd may be attended with much inconvenience.

4. Because thro' more experience, they are more prudent and discreet in conducting an intrigue to prevent suspicion. The commerce with them is therefore safer with regard to your reputation. And with regard to theirs, if the affair should happen to be known, considerate people might be rather inclin'd to excuse an old woman who would kindly take care of a young man, form his manners by her good Counsels, and prevent his ruining his health and fortune among mercenary prostitutes.

5. Because in every animal that walks upright, the deficiency of the fluids that fill the muscles appears first in the highest part: The Face first grows lank and wrinkled; then the neck; then the breast and arms; the lower parts continuing to the last as plump as ever: So that covering all

above with a basket, and regarding to only what is below the girdle, it is impossible of two women to know an old from a young one. And as in the dark all cats are grey, the pleasure of corporal enjoyment with an old woman is at least equal, and frequently superior, every knack being by practice capable of omprovement.

6. Because the sin is less. The debauching a virgin may be her ruin, and make her for life unhappy.

7. Because the compunction is less. The having made a young girl miserable may give you frequent bitter reflections; none of which can attend the making an old woman happy.
8thly and lastly, they are so grateful!!

Thus much for my paradox. But still I advise you to marry directly; being sincerely your affectionate friend,
Benjamin Franklin[18]

The reason for trouncing on these men's reputations is that you might know the truth. Unless you are young, the history you learned was severely sanitized in order not to offend the scruples of previous generations. If you are young, please understand that your textbooks have been modified so as to create, out of you, an unpaid, underfed communist worker.

---

[18] "Founders Online: Old Mistresses Apologue, 25 June 1745." *National Archives and Records Administration*, National Archives and Records Administration, founders.archives.gov/documents/Franklin/01-03-02-0011.

FAMOUS WORSHIPFUL MASTERS in U.S. included Benjamin Franklin and George Washington. Franklin, first Grand Master of Pennsylvania, also joined Paris Lodge when he was ambassador to France, helped to initiate Voltaire into Masonry. Washington, Worshipful Master of Alexandria, Va. Lodge, was zealous Mason for 47 years. Some Masons started a movement to make him national Grand Master of all U.S. Masons, to be united into a national grand Lodge. But Massachusetts Masons did not consent and the idea died.

DECEIVING AMERICA
Jesuits and Masons in the Church

America, populated for the most part by a Christian people, was given an evil government, for an evil purpose. These evil men with an evil purpose were among the brightest of their day. More than that, there is considerable evidence that they had supernatural help from evil beings. Because they were smart and because the very pillars of Masonry were formed by Jesuits, these men, unsaved and ungodly as they may have been, knew the Gospel. They also knew human nature. They were students of the first order. The one thing they knew was that, if their perverted doctrine was to take hold in America, it had to sound Christian and it had to sound Protestant.

I must remind you here that it is the Devil who offered Jesus wealth and power if he would worship him. *The Devil's side is always going to be better funded than the church.* The Masons were wealthy businessmen. They brought wealth, status, power and education with them from England. The "simple" Christians in the Colonies were no match for these men. These men paid for our church buildings and served as our Elders and Deacons. Often, they supported the whole local church. Any independent, God fearing rebels were quickly silenced. These men started schools of higher learning. They started, funded, and taught in the nation's seminaries, be they Baptist, Anglican, Methodist or Presbyterian. America's pastors learned their doctrine from these men, and that doctrine was twisted.

This is the lie:

That God Almighty was uniting men and women from every tribe, tongue and nation, on this new continent, that he was forming a new nation, with a new culture and a single language, for his Glory.

Lucifer's quest has always been to undo Babel.

Here are a few of the lies taught to the church:
1. Providence refers to your God.
2. The Great Architect of the Universe refers to Jehovah.
3. God has given every individual the right to seek happiness.
4. Freedom is a right, guaranteed by God.
5. Bloody warfare is of God and a primary means to attain God's will.

Providence was a word almost never used by Christians. However, it is in almost every government document from the era, Providence was used by a Deist to refer to their impersonal god. Providence had, according to the Deists, created everything, including man. Providence had, "Established governments among men."

The Great Architect of the Universe is a Masonic term and always refers to Osiris. It is never used in the church to refer to Jehovah God.

The Pursuit of Happiness is not guaranteed by God. Happiness is found in a right relationship with God through Jesus Christ. For a pagan to seek happiness may be natural but it is not a promise of God and apart from Christ, happiness is futile or fleeting at best.

Freedom is not a right guaranteed by Yahweh. The New Testament not only does not guarantee freedom, it commands slaves to be obedient to their masters. Paul called himself a slave of Jesus Christ. Jesus said that anyone who does not deny himself, take up his cross and follow him, is not worthy of him.

Only in America has Freedom ever been called a Christian's right.

"Slaves, be obedient to those who are your masters according to the flesh, with fear and trembling, in the sincerity of your heart, as to Christ..."

(Ephesians 6:5)

"Slaves, in all things obey those who are your masters on earth, not with external service, as those who merely please men, but with sincerity of heart, fearing the Lord."

(Colossians 3:22)

"All who are under the yoke as slaves are to regard their own masters as worthy of all honor so that the name of God and our doctrine will not be spoken against.."

(1 Timothy 6:1)

"Slaves are to submit to their own masters in everything, to be well-pleasing, not argumentative..." Titus 2:9

"Servants, submit yourselves to your masters with all respect, not only to those who are good and gentle, but even to those who are unreasonable."

(1 Peter 2:18)

NOTE: No other point of Scripture is considered so *"Unamerican"* or so *"Politically Incorrect."* I would invite you to argue with God himself. Perhaps you may change his mind.

Bloody warfare results from Babel and Babel was the result of sin and rebellion. There are reasons for war. On occasion there may be a just cause for war; however, most of the reasons for war are aimed at making the rich richer and accomplishing a satanic goal. In the case of the American Revolution, it was to provide the bloodshed and pain, required by Lucifer, from those who would serve him. Like Canada, America could have accomplished it with a treaty, but the United States of America is not Canada. The United States serves a greater purpose, and it had to be birthed in pain and blood.

In America, a land peopled by God's children, Lucifer found a nation that would undo Babel, once again uniting the world under a single culture, flag and language. This was just a beginning.

This will be a phoenix, destined to crash and burn. Out of the flames and the fire of America will come the New World Order that will defeat the Saints and make Lucifer the god of this world forever... And, they *will* sell this whole idea to the church.

Fools we were...

Mark Twain said, "It is easier to fool people than to convince them that they have been fooled."[19]

That isn't Scripture, but it is a truism. We were lied to from birth by parents, school teachers, Sunday School teachers, pastors, Bible school teachers and Seminary professors... all of whom were repeating lies that they had been taught... lies that they believed, with all their heart, to be Gospel Truth...

It takes the Spirit of the Living God to help us break out of that level of demonic deception.

How much Masonic Doctrine has been foisted on us, marketed as Scriptural Truth or Historical Fact?

---

[19] "A Quote by Mark Twain." *Goodreads*, Goodreads, www.goodreads.com/quotes/584507-it-s-easier-to-fool-people-than-to-convince-them-that.

- How could we have believed that salvation came by walking an aisle, shaking the preacher's hand and repeating a magic little prayer?
- How could we have believed that praying that prayer gave us the right to live the rest of our lives as we pleased and go to heaven when we died?
- How did "Take up your cross and follow me" morph into "If you tithe, God will make you rich and fill your life with material blessings"?
- How could we have believed that it was God giving us stuff to store up in barns while his dearest children suffered, starved and died everywhere but here?
- Why did we never question Christmas Trees or Easter Bunnies that laid eggs?
- How could we have believed that statues of a pagan goddess were acceptable, patriotic symbols of liberty?
- How could we have believed that Benjamin Franklin, America's first publisher of pornography and faithful member of secret societies at home and abroad was a Christian man?
- Why did we never ask questions about Thomas Jefferson, who cut out, moved around and pasted passages in his Bible until it agreed with his beliefs?
- Why did we not ask questions concerning George Washington, who always walked out of church before communion and never participated… a man whose own Pastor claimed was a deist and not a Christian?
- What about our Nation's Capital? First named Rome and laid out exactly like the city in Italy? The name was changed to Washington DC… and no one remembers Rome?

- What about the streets of Washington, laid out in an unfinished pentagram?
- What about the *Pentagon,* headquarters of our military?
- What about a phallic symbol representing the missing organ of Osiris? How could we have believed that an Egyptian Phallic Symbol was simply an innocent monument, built in honor of a *godly* President?
- What about the reflecting pond representing the birth canal of Isis?
- What about the Capitol Dome with the Pagan goddess atop... the Dome that represents the womb of Isis?
- How could we fail to notice that Washington DC was a clone of Rome, the capitol of pagan idolatry for the whole world?
- What about the pagan Egyptian imagery that decorates our Dollar Bill? How could it be that we never noticed, remarked or complained?
- How did we justify the genocide of the Native Americans or make heroes of the Cavalry that slaughtered them?
- Why did we never question the City of Washington being in the District of the Goddess Columbia?

All these were sold to us as part, and parcel, of a Christian nation. It has been taught in our schools. Everybody believed it. If we had suspected that something was wrong, if we had stated our misgivings, we would have been outcasts of society.

God is separating the sheep from the goats. The sheep are waking up and the scales are falling from their eyes. The goats march on, in blissful ignorance, convinced that they are Christians, living in a Christian nation, and that God has given them money to store up in barns because they sent money to a TV Evangelist.

I am hurt that so many people I once looked up to as "Super Sheep" have turned out to be "Stupid Goats," embracing abortion, sodomy and Chrislam...

If you are a goat, there is hope. You can be born again as a sheep. When you find Jesus, the scales will fall off and you will understand...

If you are a sheep, take up your *cross* and follow Jesus.

It is amazing the level of deceit that has been foisted into the church. How could I have believed that it was God's will that my friends went to Vietnam, killed others, and were killed, because it was America's war? There was no doubt even allowed that it was not only America's war, it was God's war!

It has been written that Abraham Lincoln accepted Jesus at Gettysburg. I would hope so. But the documentation is a little shaky. He is the hero... God's man in the Civil War. All I can do is note that little saying, *"Winners write the history books."* (You know there were Southern Generals who, if you use your Bible as the judge, were better Christians than Lincoln.)

Lincoln's Emancipation Proclamation specifically excludes the part of Virginia that touches Washington.[20]

Lincoln's Emancipation Proclamation specifically excludes the part of Virginia that touches Washington, the place where his friends and many members of congress had their houses and farms. Did you know that? Was that even in your college textbook?

If you were to read *Morals and Dogma* by Albert Pike, you would learn some of the occultic reasons for that war. If that war had not been fought, and American blood spilled, it is doubtful that we would be talking about the New World Order from America. From the Battles of Lexington and Concord, to the Oracle of Damascus, there is always an occultic reason for bloodshed: it *always* benefits the rich and powerful. Those who would bow down, and worship Lucifer are only too happy to sacrifice the blood of unnamed heroes.

The Masonic motto, ordo ab chao, *order out of chaos* and the motto on the American dollar bill, e pluribus unum, *out of many, one*, speak to Lucifer's longstanding goal of restoring the Kingdom of Nimrod, now known as the New World Order to pagans and the Kingdom of the Antichrist to Christians.

I keep remembering Ingersoll Lockwood's Baron Trump novels. These works described Donald Trump to a tee… Ingersoll followed those with a novel called, *The Last President*. These were, according to the publisher's foreword, a work of Memetic Occultism. Am I an occultist? Of course not, but as a Bible believer, I do believe that there is a very real devil who has very real plans and who shares those plans with those who would bow down and worship him.

What I am saying is that the deception is real, and the danger is to believers who will not open their eyes and pay attention. What has

---

[20] *Virginia-Maryland Boundary for Chesapeake Bay/Eastern Shore,* www.virginiaplaces.org/boundaries/wvboundary.html.

happened is a grave deception and the church bought it. What is coming is called in the Bible the Great Delusion. The Church in America, already deceived, is being deluded.

American Government was never Christian. It was designed, not according to Scripture, but according to the "New Atlantis" vision of Sir Francis Bacon.[21]

One must ask the question. If the idea for the United States as a precursor to the New World Order did not come from the Bible, where did it come from? The answer is found in a novel, *The New Atlantis, A Work Unfinished. by Sir Francis Bacon, Lord Verulam, Viscount of St. Alban.* The book was published in 1659. It details the founding of a new nation called the New Atlantis. That nation is Babylon reborn, Babel undone, and the United States of America, all rolled into one. I would think that you would have learned this in school. Did you learn that in school?

---

[21] "THE NEW ATLANTIS." *Alice's Adventures in Wonderland, by Lewis Carroll*, Project Gutenberg, www.gutenberg.org/files/2434/2434-h/2434-h.htm.

The Masonic motto, ORDO AB CHAO and the motto on your Dollar bill, E PLURIBUS UNUM, Order out of Chaos, and Out of Many; One, speak to Lucifer's longstanding goal of restoring the Kingdom of Nimrod, now known as the New World Order to pagans and the Kingdom of the Antichrist to Christians.

It would be easy at this point to forget the theme of this book, *Lucifer's Quest; Undoing Babel*. For some five thousand years, Lucifer's mission has been to heal the wound he was dealt at Babel. If it were not for that simple key, much of what I write here might have remained locked. Perhaps you and I could have never put all these different things together.

Never forget Lucifer's quest.

NEW

ATLANTIS.

A Work unfinished.

Written by the Right Honorable, FRANCIS,
Lord *Verulam*, *Viscount* St. *Alban*.

L O N D O N,
Printed by *Tho: Newcomb*, 1659.

PART THREE

THE PRESENT

THE CATHOLIC – ISLAMIC CONNECTION

Alberto Rivera, an ex-Jesuit, first told the story of Mohammad's wife: "'Teachers were sent to young Muhammad and he had intensive training. Muhammad studied the works of St. Augustine which prepared him for his "great calling." The Vatican had Catholic Arabs across North Africa spread the story of a great one who was about to rise up among the people and be the chosen one of their God."

"A rich Catholic widow was sent to Mohammed to help guide him."

A wealthy Arabian lady who was a faithful follower of the pope played a tremendous part in this drama. She was a widow named Khadijah. She gave her wealth to the church and retired to a convent but was given an assignment. She was to find a brilliant young man who could be used by the Vatican to create a new religion and become the messiah for the children of Ishmael."[22]

---

[22] "The Creation of the Prophet Muhammad." *Religion vs. Spirituality - What's The Difference?*, www.bibliotecapleyades.net/vatican/esp_vatican33.htm.

Muslim women dressed in mock Catholic habits... all around the world? Try explaining that one!

There is no reason to doubt the story told by Rivera. So very much of what he said has been proven to be true and it fits. Mary, the only woman mentioned in the Qur'an is mentioned 33 times. How else do you explain that?

It is my belief (not a Word from God) that following the great defeat of Islam, the Pope will make a great revelation and a wonderful offer to take all the world's Muslims back into the fold and that they will, with very few exceptions, take him up on the offer. This will be one more step in the unification of the world's religions.

The global elite, with help from our own government, planted demolition explosives in the world trade center, hired and trained muslims to fly planes into the towers and set off the explosives, bringing the towers down.

Why are the Muslims angry? Why would they want to attack and kill us?

Do you really want to know?

This was done to justify a war that would take the oil away from the Arabs and give it to the Luciferian Elite.

We used the 9/11 attack to justify an invasion that has brought down nations, sparked Islamic Terror and killed or displaced millions of people.

Why are the Muslims angry? If people from another nation and culture bombed your home, village and nation, killed your parents and your children and left you homeless, living in a tent in a refugee camp, would you be angry?

The Luciferian Elite are intent on destroying the United States, Europe and all of Western Civilization so that they may build their New World Order... what the Bible calls "The Kingdom of the Beast." For that reason, they are giving very angry Muslims the opportunity to go to Europe and the United States where they will wreak vengeance on those who have destroyed everything they ever knew and killed almost everyone they ever loved...

Yes, there is a religious side to their fight and yes, the Koran does instruct them to kill the unbeliever. But this religious fervor is being fueled by a hatred for the people who attacked them, destroyed their lands and killed their people. They were defending their own homes and their own families. We labeled them terrorists and rebels.

A man who takes up a gun and defends his own house, family and village against an invading army is neither a terrorist nor a rebel, he is a father, a friend and a patriot.

This is the ugly truth that leaves me standing in tears and disbelief as the American Church, lost in a Masonic lie, sides with our government and finds its only hope in the United States of America and the vain and empty hope that God will somehow use Donald Trump to save us.

We offer the blood of a million babies a year to Baal. We have rejected the God of our fathers and opened our arms to every pagan god that has ever existed. We glorify sodomy and sexual perversion. We conduct wars, based on false flag events, killing and hurting millions... in a fight over oil.

Then Jesus said to His disciples, "If anyone wants to come with Me, he must deny himself, take up his cross, and follow Me. Matthew 16:24

You can wave the flag, or you can take up your cross and follow Jesus... you cannot do both.

If you take up your cross and follow Jesus, you are an enemy of the State.

If you wave a flag and pledge your support to the government of the United States, you are an enemy of the cross and of the God of Abraham, Isaac and Jacob.

It is that simple, really!

THE FAITH OF MILLIONS

The Religion of the Pope and the Pope of the Religion

CATHOLICISM

It is my strongest belief that Pope Francis is and will continue to be a major player in the End Times scenario. I will have much to say about the man and his role, but it is necessary to first examine the religion of the Pope.

In his book The Faith of Millions, John O'Brien, a Catholic priest and full Professor of Theology at Notre Dame, explains the procedure of the mass:

"When the priest pronounces the tremendous words of consecration, he reaches up into the heavens, brings Christ down from His throne, and places Him upon our altar to be offered up again as the victim for the sins of man. It is a power greater than that of monarchs and emperors: it is greater than that of saints and angels, greater than that of Seraphim and Cherubim. Indeed, it is greater even than the power of

124

the Virgin Mary. While the Blessed Virgin was the human agency by which Christ became incarnate a single time, the priest brings Christ down from heaven, and renders Him present on our altar as the eternal Victim for the sins of man—not once but a thousand times! The priest speaks and lo! Christ, the eternal and omnipotent God, bows His head in humble obedience to the priest's command."[23]

Scripture says:

For the Messiah did not enter a sanctuary made with hands (only a model of the true one) but into heaven itself, so that He might now appear in the presence of God for us. He did not do this to offer Himself many times, as the high priest enters the sanctuary yearly with the blood of another. Otherwise, He would have had to suffer many times since the foundation of the world. But now He has appeared one time, at the end of the ages, for the removal of sin by the sacrifice of Himself. And just as it is appointed for people to die once—and after this, judgment— so also the Messiah, having been offered once to bear the sins of many, will appear a second time, not to bear sin, but to bring salvation to those who are waiting for Him. (Hebrews 9:24-28 HCSB)

Someone, *please help me...*

As politically incorrect as it may be, let me state that the Catholic Church is not a Christian church; not even an apostate church. The organization has never been and never will be Christian.

In the story of Osiris that we have previously covered, you understand that somehow, sometime, in a way we may not understand, Lucifer heard the basics of the planned redemption of mankind. The book of Job tells us that the Devil had free access to Heaven and

---

[23] O'Brien, John Anthony. *The Faith of Millions.* Our Sunday Visitor Press, 1938.

conversed with God himself. It is not hard to imagine that he would hear hints about a coming virgin birth. To this day, the Devil has never had an original thought. Everything he does, is a duplication from what he either heard from God or saw God do.

The story of Osiris is the virgin birth, poorly executed by the Devil. Lucifer thought that he would get the jump on God and do it first. By the time Lucifer gave the Emperor Constantine a dream and a flag, the whole world, in one way or another, worshiped a god and his son. Whether they called his name in Egyptian, Greek or Latin, most of the world worshiped Horus and his mother, Isis. Christians, who were multiplying like nuts worshiped Jesus. Jesus, like Horus, was both God and the Son of God. The similarities were amazing.

And so, led by the light of Lucifer, the Emperor gave the order that the whole world should be baptized, and he declared that Rome would now be called the Holy Roman Empire.

Priests of Apollo and Dianna, Horus Isis and Osiris became Christian priests overnight. A new sign was painted, and the Temple of Dianna became the Temple of Mary. The Mother of God Temple did not even have to change its name. Osiris became the Father, Horus the Son, and the Bishop of Rome took the place of God on the Earth. All of the rituals surrounding the Queen of Heaven and the Mother of God were now directed at Mary, her baptismal name.

In one fell swoop, all of paganism was baptized. Every pagan god was given a Christian name and elevated to Saint. The very first thing this new "Church" did was to start burning Bible-Believing Christians at the stake. *Nothing* had changed but the names.

Finding out which Christians were saved, and which ones simply believed in the Church of Rome and its pantheon of gods became difficult. The wrong question or answer could get you tortured and killed. It was the beginning of a one thousand-year reign of terror.

I do not think you learned this in school or in church. This is how Catholic Doctrine can contradict plain Scripture and the Catholic Jesus be sacrificed thousands of times a week…but the Jesus of the Bible only once.

I am a Born again Believer in Jesus Christ. For me, the Bible is the absolute and final authority, period. I have a Christian, supernatural worldview. I believe that the Bible is literal unless proven otherwise. What I write will always reflect these foundational principles and beliefs. I cannot and will not violate the core of my being.

Where I speak of any group or system of belief, my standard is the same. Does it agree with, or contradict, the Word of God? Where any church, religion, group or individual promotes any belief or doctrine that is opposed to Scripture, I stand opposed. I can do no other. I stand opposed to multiple leaders and Pastors who would call themselves Protestant, Pentecostal or Charismatic. I published an article titled, *"The Half Gospel Heresy.* Allow me to insert that here:

THE HALF GOSPEL HERESY
THE DAMNABLE PRACTICE OF SELECTIVE PREACHING

The Half Gospel Heresy is well hidden and difficult to detect. The problem lies in the fact that no heresy is ever directly stated; everything the Half Gospel Preacher says from the pulpit is Gospel Truth and nothing preached would ever fail the test of Scriptural analysis. The finest theologian would be hard pressed to detect heresy though he were to dissect the sermon line by line. The insidiousness of this heresy lies in what is never preached, that which is never spoken.

These men preach Jesus as Savior but never as Lord, Heaven without Hell, Salvation without repentance, blessing without suffering and Gifts of the Spirit without Fruit of the Spirit. They revel in stories of Peter and James being freed from prison, but they will never mention Stephen being stoned, James losing his head or Peter being crucified upside down. Altar calls are for blessing and healing but never for repentance or salvation. Congregants are encouraged to worship but not to be holy, speak in tongues but not to be saved, get close to God but not to renounce sin, be free from worry but not free from sin. When these Heretics talk about the woman caught in adultery, they always speak of forgiveness but never read the part that says, "Go and sin no more." They speak of how the saints overcame by the Blood of the Lamb and the word of their testimony but never read the third verse in the trilogy... the one that says, "they loved not their lives unto death."

Theirs is an all-inclusive Gospel; bring in everybody, accept everybody, encourage everybody to sing and praise and worship. At the same time, it is a non-confrontational Gospel... sinners are never confronted with their sin and never come under conviction. They are encouraged to accept Jesus but never asked to repent or walk away from or reject their sin. It is a Gospel that lets you feel good in your sin. It is a church where you can bring your live-in girlfriend or your same sex lover and worship God with no fear of judgment or conviction of sin. This Half-Gospel heresy lets you go to church and worship every Sunday for decades and go to Hell when you die.

Every word of every sermon is true but by selecting the passages never to read and the subjects never to preach, these Heretics damn well-meaning church members... good people, to a Devil's Hell. When is the last time your Pastor's sermon brought conviction to your soul and drove you to the altar to repent? That may be the most important question you face today; the wrong answer should have you asking God to lead you to a Whole-Gospel Church.

This is a stinging critique that could only be applied to Protestant Churches. Am I anti-Protestant? Where they abandon plain Scripture, yes.

I taught English in Mexico for two years. Two of my students were Roman Catholic Priests. They were Professors in the Catholic Seminary a few blocks from the school where I taught. We became friends. I would often eat lunch with them at the Seminary. We started out with the premise that we could discuss anything but with the foregone conclusion that no one was going to convert the other. We had hours of friendly, if sometimes heated debate. I came away with a basic understanding; the Roman Catholic Church does not accept the Bible as its ultimate authority.

For the Catholic Priest, the Bible is one authority among several. The Bible is the "Word of God," but so is Cannon Law, the findings of Church Councils and the words of the Pope, spoken "Ex-Cathedra." If Church tradition contradicts the Bible, it is often accepted as a harmless tradition.

This leads to many areas in which I find myself opposed to the doctrine and practice of the Catholic Church. That does not mean that I did not appreciate and like those two Mexican gentlemen.

I make a great distinction between Catholics as people and the religious system that is the Church of Rome. I find it easy to befriend Catholics while standing opposed to the doctrines and practices of the Catholic Church. Both the Church and the people have a right to their beliefs. There are many instances in which they are convinced that I am wrong. I do not hold that against them. They will and often do, stand up to me and tell me why they believe I am wrong. I am not going to change my mind, but I respect them, and I listen to them.

Today, we have a Pope in Rome who is infuriating traditional Catholics. It is well known that an early church Bishop, Bishop Malachy, prophesied that Pope Francis would be the last Pope.

You can research the Prophecy of Saint Malachy and read it for yourself. Many Catholics stand with me in opposition to the words and deeds of Pope Francis. In this, we find common ground.

MARY, MOTHER OF GOD

A Word from Mary...

The name ISIS, shared by the Caliphate in the Middle East and the God of Fortresses or Thrones, is of utmost importance. To bypass the name is to misunderstand what is happening. It is the goddess Isis to whom Daniel referred in Daniel 11:38, where, speaking of the Antichrist, he said "Instead of them, he will honor a god of fortresses; a god unknown to his ancestors he will honor with gold and silver, with precious stones and costly gifts."

Instead of them, he will honor a god of fortresses; a god unknown to his ancestors he will honor with gold and silver, with precious stones and costly gifts. (Daniel 11:38 NIV)

Mary, the Mary of the Bible, was a young woman of tremendous faith. Her position as the birth mother of Jesus Christ was a great privilege and a source of unimaginable pain. I am certain that she has a place in Heaven among the Saints. I believe that she is near her Son's throne. That said, she is portrayed as being very human. She is neither the "Mother of God," nor is she the "Queen of Heaven." She makes no earthly appearances, grants no favours, answer no prayers and recommends no citizen of earth to her Son. The "Mary reputed to do and be all that is a pagan goddess, baptized Mary by the Catholic Church. Her titles predate the Mary of the Bible by thousands of years. Her name is Isis.

Who then is Isis? Also known as Mary, Queen of Heaven, Mother of God, Tammuz, Semiramis, Ashtoreth, Ishtar, Eostre, Isis, Venus, Aphrodite, Astarte, Kali and Ostara. It is from Ostara and Eostre that we get the English word, Easter. Isis is the Goddess of Fortresses. She was worshipped as the ideal mother and wife as well as the patroness of nature and magic.

Then he brought me to the entrance of the north gate of the house of the Lord, and I saw women sitting there, mourning the god Tammuz. (Ezekiel 8:14 NIV)

As we have repeated often, Isis married her brother, Osiris (Nimrod). Osiris was murdered by Set, cut into fourteen pieces and scattered throughout Egypt. Using her magical skills, she gathered the body parts that had been strewn about the earth by Set. His penis, however, had been swallowed by a fish and could not be recovered. Not to be outdone, Isis made an artificial phallus and impregnated herself. The child conceived was Horus. She said that Horus was Osiris reincarnated and when he was still a preteen, she married him and took him to her bed. Thus, Isis was married to both her brother and her son.

"The children gather wood, and the fathers kindle the fire, and the women knead dough to make cakes for the _queen of heaven_; and they pour out drink offerings to other gods in order to spite Me. (Jeremiah 7:18) (NASB)

The worship of Isis spread throughout Greece and then Rome, continuing until paganism was silenced by Constantine. She was called "Diana of the Ephesians" in the New Testament. In the Old Testament, she is Tammuz, for whom the women of Israel would weep. She was the "Queen of Heaven" spoken of by the Prophet Jeremiah. The paintings and statues of Isis nursing her son Horus lived on as the image of Mary nursing Jesus. Isis or Diana of the Ephesians was baptized by the Catholic Church and given the name MARY, QUEEN OF HEAVEN and later crowned "MARY, MOTHER OF GOD"!

And when they heard these sayings, they were full of wrath, and cried out, saying, Great is Diana of the Ephesians. (Acts 19:28)

Muslims, unlike Catholics, do not openly worship Mary or pray to her. This gives us an insight into Daniel's assertion that "he will honor a god of fortresses; a god unknown to his ancestors". It is becoming apparent that, while Pope Francis, serving as the False Prophet, is working to unite the world's religions, the Antichrist will join Islam to the Catholic Church, encouraging them to worship Mary, the Queen of Heaven and the god of fortresses. He will then force the whole world to worship Mary and bow down to her image.

If you are not Catholic, you may not be aware, but the world is afloat with supernatural apparitions of Mary and multiplied thousands of Mediums bring daily messages from "Mary". A Google search for, "Messages from Mary" gave 132,000,000 (that is one hundred thirty-two million) results. Mary is appearing to Muslims on a regular basis. Google gave 1,550,000 results on Messages from Mary to Muslims. According to google, abc.net.au. Millions of Muslims are seeing apparitions of Mary and are being prepped to accept the worship of Mary. A great miracle by the "Eternal Virgin," say resurrecting a dead man and calling him her son, would do the trick!

A Google search for, "Messages from Mary" gave 132,000,000 results!!

***

THE ORACLE OF DAMASCUS

A key, now in the lock...

The oracle concerning Damascus:

*"Behold, Damascus is about to be removed from being a city
And will become a fallen ruin." (Isaiah 17:1)*

A protest against Syrian president Assad in 2011 has led to the death of over 250,000 people, and displaced *eleven million* people, forcing them to leave their homes in Syria.

A friend who has spent considerable study on the above passage informs me that it is the fall of Damascus that precludes the seven-year peace treaty initiated by the Evil One. The war in Syria has gathered all the End-Time nations and players into one very small piece of land. It is no accident that this is happening on Israel's northern border. When Israel is attacked, it will be through Syria.

Damascus is the oldest, continually occupied, city in the world. Just seven years ago it was a beautiful city, one of the jewels of the Middle East. It was a great place to visit and live. You would have loved the city. Today, all but a tiny remnant of that city lies in ruin. How symbolic it is the death of the oldest city in the world that God chose as the event which will mark the beginning of the end of all things.

I am no expert on the Middle East, but I can read Scripture. As bad as the destruction is today, what is to come will be worse. Look at the passage in its context:

Prophecy about Damascus

The oracle concerning Damascus:

"Behold, Damascus is about to be removed from being a city
And will become a fallen ruin.
2 "The cities of Aroer are forsaken;
They will be for flocks to lie down in,
And there will be no one to frighten them.
3 "The fortified city will disappear from Ephraim,
And sovereignty from Damascus
And the remnant of Aram;
They will be like the glory of the sons of Israel,"
Declares the Lord of hosts.
(Isaiah 17:1-3 NASB)

The destruction will be total. The area will be abandoned. Shepherds will graze their flocks in the ruins of Damascus and the surrounding area. Perhaps the key to knowing that the oracle is fully accomplished is found in the line, *"And sovereignty from Damascus."* The day that Assad leaves Damascus or dies, the Oracle will be considered completed. I believe that that day is close at hand. Perhaps, by the time you read this book it will be finished.

Trump has now announced the withdrawal of American forces from Syria, perhaps clearing the way for the invasion prophesied in Ezekiel 38. I believe that we will be a major player in the end times. Probably not as the America you have known. It will be the same people, operating from the same places, but the Republic will be dead, replaced by something new, menacing, and evil.

I begin with Damascus because it is a sign that cannot be misinterpreted or misread. When Damascus, including the area around the palace, ceases to exist, when Sovereignty leaves Damascus and Syria, as a Sovereign nation ceases to exist, The End has come. There can be no denying of that fact.

My friend Doug Krieger says that we are in the year 5,993 Post Adam. That would place us seven years from the return of Christ and the start of the Millennial Reign of Christ.

Doug points out that we are in the seventh year of the Oracle of Damascus. God works in sevens and the conclusion of that war, and the destruction of Damascus, should be accomplished within a year.

THE MOST WONDERFUL LIE

Every up and coming Dictator has used the Liberal Left to destroy the nation he desired to control and then destroyed the liberals when he came into power. Mao, Lenin, and Hitler all encouraged Homosexuals and homosexual behavior while they were fighting for power... When they gained absolute control, they lined up all the Gays, who had so recently come out of the closet, and shot them...

So shall it be at the coming of the AntiMessiah...

The Elite have been encouraging, enabling and financing the godless Left. They have raised them to a position of incredible power, authority and glory... Amazing, considering how few Americans actually think that way...

Millions who now find it convenient and to their advantage to support the Left, are violating their own conscience to do so... When the world and the Nation swing to the Right, these people will let out a collective sigh of relief and jump on the Conservative Bandwagon...

Tens of millions of younger people are without direction or guidance... they have no idea who they are, why they are here, what they are doing or where they are going. This is a miserable state of existence... If someone comes along and offers them direction and a reason to be... they will bow down and follow him.

The AntiMessiah is going to rescue us from the godless Left. He is going to give the younger people a reason to live and a cause worth dying for...

I see the AntiMessiah as a Christ, a Messiah, a Savior... He will be exactly what the Jews were looking for in a Messiah when Jesus came. They rejected Jesus because He did not fit their picture of who and what a Messiah should be... Their Messiah was going to ride into town, gather an Army and destroy their enemies...

That, is exactly what the AntiMessiah will do, which is why the Jews who rejected Jesus Christ will embrace this new Messiah with open arms... He will be the sum of their hopes and dreams...

What you see today is the Hegelian Dialectic taken to its occultic peak... Hegel on Steroids if you would... No Messiah could come, no hero could arise unless there was an evil and unbeatable foe who threatened the very life of the common man. The Left is nothing more than an inflated target, waiting to be shot down.

I am convinced that the Man of Sin will come to save us from the Left, and evil everywhere. He will really be seen as a Savior, a Christ and a Messiah. He will be preceded by the Suffering Servant who will defeat the Enemies of Israel and prepare the way. He will rise to the Throne of Israel and it is from Jerusalem that he will rule the world.

It might not go down this way and it might not involve these people. I could be wrong... but you need to think of how it is that the deception will appeal strongly to the Church and those who identify as Christians...

I think that it will go down something like this...

There will be some kind of False Flag... more tragic than any seen before. Out of the tragedy, Trump will declare Martial Law and become absolute ruler of the United States... a man without a Constitution, promising, always, to restore Democracy when the crisis is past... Problem being, the crisis will never pass. Somewhere along the line, Trump will be assassinated, and lying in State, under the Apotheosis of Washington and the Idol to Columbia, while the Masons hold their Rising of Osiris Occult Working down the street, Osiris will be incarnated in that dead body, animate it and fake a resurrection.

Trump will be there when Russia, Turkey, Iran and the rest, invade Israel from the north. God will destroy those nations in the Mountains of Israel, and Trump will be there to take credit and force the remnant of Edom to sign a treaty that is much to their disadvantage...

Trump will encourage his Son-in-Law Jared Kushner, and Kushner, as a Son of David, will ascend to the Throne of David and then the throne of the World... Of course, the Pope is right in there, and no Treaty can be made without the approval and participation of the Vatican. They will all work together...

The chances that it will go down exactly like that, are about a hundred to none against it... It won't happen exactly like that, but you need to jump out of your little box and start thinking, praying and watching...

It is not going to go down like it happened in the Left Behind Series, and it will not even resemble what the Prophecy teachers were saying back in the Seventies... If your eyes are open, your Lamp full of Oil, and you are watching... you will see and not be fooled. Otherwise, you will be made a fool...

Please Pray, watch and think... You do not want to believe the lie...

Hegelian Dialectic

Agenda
Centralization of
power

↙

Thesis
Manufactured terrorist
threat

→

Anti-Thesis
Repressive police
state

↙

Synthesis
Removal of freedoms, transfer of power from
the many to the few

For those unfamiliar with Hegel, imagine a pendulum... We elect a Democrat to fix what the Republican has messed up. The Democrat messes up. The Republican promises to fix the problem if we only give up a little freedom. We elect the Republican and give up a little freedom. The Republican messes up and the Democrat promises to fix it if we will only give up a little freedom... Etcetera, etcetera, etcetera, ad nauseum

CANDADATES FOR ANTIMESSIAH

There are certainly thousands of people who could be added to my list. I am going to list my top six. It is more than possible that someone not on my list will become "The Antichrist." That notwithstanding, these six are Antichrist as in they stand against Jesus Christ of the Bible.

There is an Assyrian. There is a bad man in the Middle East. There is a Roman and a Babylonian… Even a Russian may be found by some. My understanding is that there are many bad men. We have a beast with many heads. One head destroys three heads and the rest submit to him… The guy who wins becomes the Antichrist… If you see one Man of Sin and many antichrists, you get the picture.

I want to talk about each of the individuals on my list, one at a time. First, it is necessary to state that I am a firm believer that the United States of America is the End Times Babylon. Peter called Rome the Babylon of his day. If that was true, on the same grounds and in the same way I will identify the United States as the Babylon of our day. I do not have time to offer proofs here, but many are to be found on my Blog and on the Internet. This is to be understood as a constant in my understanding of the roles of the individuals on my list.

She who is in Babylon, chosen together with you, sends you her greetings, and so does my son Mark.   *1 Peter 5:13 NIV*

CANDADATE # 7

Vladimir Putin - RUSSIA
WHY? AND WHY NOT?

Putin is certainly an evil man, but Russia is eliminated from the playbook during the Ezekiel 38 war... The Armies of Magog are absolutely crushed when they attack Israel, along with their, soon to be dead, Islamic co-conspirators. Putin may survive, but he will be isolated and powerless...

CANDADATE # 6

Recep Tayyip Erdoğan - TURKEY
WHY? AND WHY NOT?

It is certain that Mr. Erdoğan of Turkey is one of the most evil and satanic men on earth It is looking as if he is set to take charge of a revived Ottoman Empire. His ghoulish appearance and nature have placed him at the top of the list of Antichrist Candidates by many who are looking for an Islamic Antichrist.

There is a problem with that, however. If you read of the war in Ezekiel 38 and 39, you find that the Army of Turkey is totally destroyed by God Almighty. The Turkish people are the descendants of Esau... the closest relatives the man has living today. There is a direct and undisputed line between Esau and Recep Tayyip Erdoğan. This is important because Obadiah 1:18 tells us, "And the house of Jacob shall be fire and the house of Joseph a flame, and the house of Esau shall become stubble, and they shall ignite them and consume them, and the house of Esau shall have no survivors, for the Lord has spoken."

Obadiah 1:18 And the house of Jacob shall be fire and the house of Joseph a flame, and the house of Esau shall become stubble, and they shall ignite them and consume them, and the house of Esau shall have no survivors, for the Lord has spoken.

It would be very hard for a dead man to become Antichrist.

CANDIDATE # 5

POPE FRANCIS – THE VATICAN
WHY? AND WHY NOT?

Two time periods have been of great interest to the whole world as of late, December of 2012 and September of 2015. Everyone had a theory of what would happen during those two time periods. Almost none of those visions came true at the appointed times. However, two events that snuck under the radar, and for the most part are tied together with an unbreakable bond.

These actual events, one tied to **December 2012** and the other to **September 2015**, should really grab your attention.

First, let us review why the whole world was looking at these dates.

DECEMBER 2012:

- God works on a different calendar. December 21st, 2012 fell on 8 Tevet 5773. The year 5773 started on 1 Tishri or September 17, 2012 and ended on 29 Elul or September 4, 2013. Let us use that Jewish year for the purposes of our discussion.
- The Zohar, written by Jews 700 years ago, claimed that in the Jewish year 5773, the Antichrist would be revealed.
- The Mayan Calendar ended in the Year 5773 with the return of their "Flying Dragon" god, Kulkulkan.
- The Aztec Calendar ended in the year 5773 with the return of their "Flying Dragon" god, Quetzalcoatl.
- The Cherokee Indian Calendar ended in 5773 with the return of their "Flying Rattlesnake" god.
- The Hindu Kali Yuga Calendar ended in 5773 at the end of the age of the "Male Demon".
- Jonathan Edwards tied, the arrival of the Antichrist and the Great Tribulation to 2012 (or 5773)
- In 1878, Dr. William J. Reid, a highly acclaimed Minister in the Presbyterian Church, wrote, "…we are prepared to answer the question, 'When will the Papal system come to an end? …in the year 2012."
- The thousand-year-old Prophecy of St. Malachy predicted that Pope Francis would be "The last Pope" a man who will usher in the Tribulation and whose reign will end with the coming of the "Terrible Judge."

- Using math and Astronomy far above my head David Flynn, in his scholarly work *CYDONIA*, claimed that the Platonic year changed on 8 Tevet 5773 and we, measured by astronomy and not astrology, entered the Age of Aquarius on that day.

So, what happened at that time?

We know that right before Christmas, in the same time frame as the **December 21st, 2012** end of the Mayan Calendar; there was a terrible Coup in the Vatican that **forced the resignation of Benedict XVI**. The resignation was not announced until February of 2013 and did not take effect until the end of that month, but the deed was done in the year 5773.

The "Last Pope" was installed on Tuesday, March 26, 2013, In the Jewish Year, 5773.

SEPTEMBER 2015

All eyes were on September of 2015 because of the end of the Shemitah and the four Blood Moons. Nothing earth shattering happened on that particular day as many had expected. The night of the last Blood Moon, many were expecting something to happen that would shake the world. When nothing of that magnitude happened, many were disappointed.

So, did nothing happen at that time? Yes, something *very prophetic happened*. It was quiet. It slipped in right under our nose. Many Christians picked up on it the instant it happened, but most never saw it at all.

Jesus, in John 5:43, said, *"I have come in My Father's name, yet you don't accept Me. If someone else comes IN HIS OWN NAME, you will accept him."*

"IN HIS OWN NAME"

On September 25th, 2015, the largest group of Heads of State, ever assembled together in one place, in the history of the world, was at the United Nations in New York.

Pope Francis stood before that group and the world. In his opening remarks, the Pontiff said, out of his own mouth, *"Thank you for your kind words. Once again, following a tradition by which I feel honored, the Secretary General of the United Nations has invited the Pope to address this distinguished assembly of nations. IN MY OWN NAME..."*

"IN MY OWN NAME..."
- Who is it who has rejected the Christian façade of Catholicism and returned to its pagan roots?
- Who is it that seeks to cause all religions to reject the doctrines that divide them?
- Who is it who seeks to unite the whole world under the pagan religion of Sumer, Babylon, Egypt and Rome?

POPE FRANCIS!

CANDADATE # 4

JARED KUSHNER – THE UNTED STATES
WHY? AND WHY NOT?

Mr. Kushner is famous because he is married to the President's daughter. He is an observant Jew and his wife converted to Judaism when they were married. He is Donald Trump's first and foremost contact with Israel and the Jews. He is known for having spent a fortune to have the address of his building changed to 666. He is an envoy to Israel from the United States. This puts him solidly in the team of the Antichrist. I can see the possibility that his Father-In-Law having prepared the way, Mr. Kushner, as a son of David, could step into the office of Man of Sin. I did not find that likely but watching him during President Trump's State of the Union Address, I changed my mind. He almost certainly will play a major role in the establishment of the New World Order.

CANDADATE # 3

HILLARY CLINTON- THE UNITED STATES

WHY? AND WHY NOT?

Since the Man of Sin of Scripture is referred to in the masculine gender, Ms. Clinton cannot be "The Man of Sin." However, she is evil enough to make the list. One of her major functions was to get Donald Trump elected… a job she carried out with a flair. If it had not been for Hillary, Trump could not have won. There is something more nefarious however…

Quoting Wikipedia here, this story is upheld by many and multiple sources. "The Babalon Working was a series of magic ceremonies or rituals performed from January to March 1946 by author, pioneer rocket-fuel scientist, and occultist Jack Parsons and Scientology founder L. Ron Hubbard. This ritual was essentially designed to manifest an individual incarnation of the archetypal divine feminine called Babalon. The project was based on the ideas of Aleister Crowley, and his description of a similar project in his 1917 novel Moonchild. " Jack

Parsons reported that the working was successful, and that Babalon had been formed in the womb of a woman who would give birth to the goddess incarnate.

In 1948, when the child would have been about a year old, Mr. Parsons reported that the spirit of the child had visited him. He reported that her name was "Hilarion". This is interesting because the name Hilarion is an ancient form of the modern name Hillary. You must ask yourself how many women named Hillary were born in 1947 and have grown to be world leaders and militant feminists.

This makes Hillary a prime candidate for Team Antichrist...

CANDADATE # 2

BARACK OBAMA – THE UNITED STATES
WHY? AND WHY NOT?

And he said unto them, I beheld Satan as בָּרָק *(Baraq) fall from heaven.*

(Luke 10:18)

...and the world hangs by a thread.

Mr. Obama is one of the most openly and obviously evil individuals on the face of the earth. There was a time when I was convinced that he would be the Antichrist. I believe that we have not seen the last of the man and that he will play an important role in the assent of the Antichrist.

BARAQ

Strong's Concordence# 1300: baraq

Transliteration: baraq
Phonetic Spelling: (baw-rawk')
  Short Definition: lightning
  Barack in Arabic is lightening.
  Barack in Aramaic is Lightening

From the Quran:
"Never doeth Allah change the condition of a people, excepting they change themselves, and Allah intendeth evil for all people, and there is no stopping him. Neither doeth he accept an equal. Barack is he who showeth you the face of Allah, giving a fear and a hope, though heavy the clouds and the thunder, exalt and prostrate to him, for even angels fear him, for he sendeth forth thunderbolts, striking whom he wills, while they dispute before the face of Allah, and he is severe in his attack. To him alone are the prayers in truth." – Quran Surah "the Barack" or *"the lightening" 13:11b-14a*

In Aramaic, which Jesus spoke, he said, *"Barack is Lightening."* When Jesus said, *"I saw Satan fall as lightening"*, *"fall like lightening"*, transliterated from the Aramaic is **barack o bama**…

Now we have Satan who fell like Barack and The World Ruler, as the most powerful men in Babylon, competing to be the most powerful men in the world, to rule the world from the New Babylon.

The one thing that stands against him is his obvious and open bent towards the demonic and evil. It may be pointed out that the Man of Sin described in the Bible will be able to fool the church and, if it were possible, even the elect. There is no way that Obama could fool the Elect… they could smell the sulfur a mile away.

The next thing is that the Antichrist will support Israel, build the Temple and sit in it. I cannot imagine Mr. Obama fulfilling that role.

CANDADATE # 1

DONALD TRUMP- THE UNITED STATES
The King of Babylon

THE DONALD: Let us start with the very name. Names are usually appropriate to the person identified with the moniker. That was especially true in the Bible. It is truer in some cultures than others, but even today, we should examine the names of the powerful.

Donald – Scottish, Gaelic: *World Ruler*.

WORLD RULER
Not everyone named Donald will be a world ruler, but when a man named Donald becomes a world ruler, one might take notice.

With Donald Trump we have a strange title that has been used for many years and in many places to identify Donald Trump. He has, for years, been called, "The Donald."

The word *the* placed in front of a noun makes that noun singular, one of a kind, and separate. Even if you are not a grammar major, you understand the difference between Donald and *The Donald* indicates that he is different, one of a kind, set apart,

Put that together with the clear meaning of the word Donald, and it makes a huge difference!

We go from "World Ruler" to "*The* World Ruler." Can you hear the difference?

ON BARON TRUMP'S MARVELOUS UNDERGROUND JOURNEY

BOOKS BY INGERSOLL LOCKWOOD

Ingersoll Lockwood wrote two very profound, and perhaps prophetic, books: *Baron Trump's Marvellous Underground Journey*, and *The Last President*.

On the title page of *The Last President*, you cannot miss: "This is a work of memetic occultism."

MEMETICS is defined as, *"a study of information based on an analogy with Darwinian evolution."*[24] Proponents describe memetics as an approach to evolutionary models of cultural information transfer. Thus, Memetic Occultism is mixing Darwinian theory with Occultic Practice as a way of predicting the future. I am glad that I saw that before I started reading *Baron Trump's Marvellous Underground Journey*. Had I not seen that, I might have passed off the Baron Trump book as a wild fairy tale or as simply children's literature.

BARON TRUMP'S MARVELLOUS UNDERGROUND JOURNEY:[25]

This book is passed off as children's literature, but it would be a hard sell today. It is a first-person's account of a magical journey taken by a boy I would assume to be in about the sixth grade. However, although the story is age appropriate for sixth graders, today's High School Graduates might have a difficult time reading and comprehending it.

This is due, I am certain, to the intentional collapse of the American Education System. Any sixth grader in 1890 could have read this.

Secondly, Darwinian Theory, Pagan Religion, and Occultic Works, form the basis for the entire story. I do not know how much of that

[24] "Memetics." *Wikipedia*, Wikimedia Foundation, 24 Dec. 2018, en.wikipedia.org/wiki/Memetics.
[25] LOCKWOOD, INGERSOLL. *Baron Trumps Marvellous Underground Journey*. 12TH MEDIA SERVICES, 2018.

would have been absorbed by a child, but to an adult who has been forewarned, it is only too obvious.

Thirdly, and lastly, little Barron Trump has the egocentric personality that only a Trump could muster. This little aristocratic brat is Donald Trump on steroids. Everything he does and says echoes the Donald Trump we know today. This boy is everything I could picture in Donald Trump as a sixth-grader. He has the attitude down. You would honestly think that the author went to elementary school with the President! I tell you the truth!

THE LAST PRESIDENT:[26]

The remarkable thing about the book called *1900*, or *THE LAST PRESIDENT*, is that it immediately follows the book on the adventures of a boy named Baron Trump.

President Bryan is a young Populist, a Democrat, and probably a closet communist. It is a short story that centers on the politics and promises of the 1890s. We get to look at what the President and the Congress do, but we get little to no insight into their persons or their lives. The book uses Memetic Occultism to predict that the Republic would collapse in the year 1900. Evidently, there was a good deal of speculation that the world, or at least the United States, would collapse in the year 1900… something that most of us can relate to a century later.

Mr. Lockwood was a wealthy Republican. As an Occultist, he firmly believed in the "Divine Right" of Kings. The heroes in his books are snobbish aristocrats and wealthy businessman. The bad guys in *The Last President*, are Democrats and socialists. They are the ones who bring an

---

[26] Lockwood, Ingersoll, et al. *The Prophetic Works of Ingersoll Lockwood: Baron Trumps Marvellous Underground Journey & 1900; or, The Last President.* Mockingbird Press, 2017.

end to the Republic in his story. *The Last President* is much more like Obama than Donald Trump.

So, what stands out here?

Ingersoll Lockwood:
1 Was an Occultist.

2. Believed in Darwinian Evolution

3. Combined Occultism and Evolution in an attempt to tell the future.

4. Taught magic and Evolution to children through his Children's Books.

5.Was an Aristocrat and a Republican.

6. Heard from Lucifer in ways he never understood.

7. Failed miserably, as the Republic did not die in 1900.

8. Telegraphed the Devil's plans more than a hundred years into the future.

Little Barron Trump:
1. Was the perfect picture of Donald Trump as a Middle Schooler.

2. Was self-absorbed, ego-centric, wealthy and aristocratic.

3. Had a huge connection with Russia and the Russians, having many connections among the rich and powerful there. Most of the story takes place in Russia.

Favourite quote:

Let me set this up. Little Baron Trump was going into dangerous territory in Northern Russia. His driver had signed on for a hundred miles and has gone that far. Little Lord Trump has told him that he will pay him double if he continues but will have him beaten by the magistrates and sent home with no money if he refuses. The poor fellow is complaining but little Trump silences him and says:

"Nay, Ivan," said I kindly, "I know no such word as cruelty
although I do confess that right seems harsh at times, but
thou wert born to serve and I to command. Providence hath
made thee poor and me rich. Do thy duty, and thou wilt find
me just and considerate. Disobey me, and thou wilt find
that this short arm may be stretched from Ilitch to
Petersburg." (The man lived in Ilitch and the Czar and
other friends of Trump lived in Petersburg.)[27]

I stand amazed at the likeness of attitude in little Barron Trump and the modern Donald Trump of today. Little Baron Trump's fascination with and connections in Russia are amazing, considering the present-day connections between the President and Russia.

To follow that up with a book called "THE LAST PRESIDENT," seems outside the realm of coincidence. It seems like the Devil was using this man who actively sought his knowledge to send a message to us.

I take out of this that Donald Trump being President in this last decade of human history is not chance, but the fulfilment of a plan hatched in Hell and known in Heaven a very long time ago. Some believe that all strong, and biblically sound, Christians should read these

---

[27] LOCKWOOD, INGERSOLL. *Baron Trumps Marvellous Underground Journey*. 12TH MEDIA SERVICES, 2018.

books. I am convinced that Satan shared his future plans with this man through his occultic works.

Weak Christians may lose their faith reading these books… If you don't know who you are in Jesus and, or, you are not grounded in the Word of God, DO NOT READ THESE BOOKS!

From fiction to fact...

I have spoken of fiction, but I shall now move to fact. I title him, "THE DONALD, The King of Babylon.

Let us be clear:
1. I am *not* saying that Donald Trump is the Antichrist.
2. I *am* saying that history, prophecy and current events, would present him as a logical candidate for the position.
3. It is perhaps more likely that he will prepare the way for the Antichrist.

Let us speak of ANTICHRIST AS MASHIACH

In the Christian world, we are expecting the Antichrist and the False Prophet. The Jews are expecting two Messiahs: *Mashiach ben David* and *Mashiach ben Yossef.* The Jewish descriptions of the two Messiahs match, almost exactly, the description of the Antichrist and the False Prophet in Christian writings and Scripture.

The very word *"Christ"* is the Greek translation of the Hebrew word Messiah. Therefore, it is quite valid to write the title Antichrist as Antimessiah. It is the same exact word.

In Jewish thought, the two Messiahs work together to bring the whole world into subjection to Israel and to Yahweh. It is a very big part of the Jewish story that one of the two Mashiachs will be killed and resurrected by the other. It is strange but true. Scripture speaks of the Antichrist as being wounded in the head with a fatal blow yet living. How can you miss the connection?

The Jews do not accept the Christian interpretation of the two distinctly different descriptions of the Messiah found in Zechariah. Christians see one Messiah coming twice, the first time as the suffering servant and the second time as the King of Kings and Lord of Lords. The Jews see two different men, one the suffering servant and the other the Great King. By the way, they see them as very human, not God at all. According to Jewish tradition, after their conquest of the world, both will grow old and die in Jerusalem.

- Jewish tradition speaks of two redeemers, each one called Mashiach. Both are involved in ushering in the Messianic era. They are Mashiach ben David and Mashiach ben Yossef.

- The term Mashiach unqualified always refers to Mashiach ben David (Mashiach the descendant of David) of the tribe of Judah. He is the actual (final) redeemer who shall rule in the Messianic age.

- Mashiach ben Yossef (Mashiach the descendant of Joseph) of the tribe of Ephraim (son of Joseph), is also referred to as Mashiach ben Ephrayim, Mashiach the descendant of Ephraim. He will come first, before the final redeemer, and later will serve as his viceroy.

- The essential task of Mashiach ben Yossef is to act as precursor to Mashiach ben David: he will prepare the world for the coming of the final redeemer…

- The principal and final function ascribed to Mashiach ben Yossef is of political and military nature. He shall wage war against the forces of evil that oppress Israel. More specifically, he will do battle against Edom, the descendants of Esau. Edom is the comprehensive designation of the enemies of Israel, and it will be crushed through the progeny of Joseph. Thus, it was prophesied of old, *"The House of Jacob will be a fire and the House of Joseph a flame, and the House of Esau for stubble."* (Obadiah 1:18): 'the progeny of

Esau shall be delivered only into the hands of the progeny of Joseph.'"[28]

Please note, in many Jewish sources, *Mashiach ben Yossef* is murdered but resurrected by *Mashiach ben David* and that is how the Jews recognize him as their Mashiach.

When the Rabbis in Israel say that Trump is preparing the way for the Mashiach, they are saying that Trump is, in their opinion, Mashiach Ben Yossef.

- Ben Yossef is from Ephraim. In Ezekiel 37:15-28 God had Ezekiel explain that the northern and southern kingdoms (called Ephraim and Judah) would one day be reunited into one nation again with David as their king. Therefore, Ephraim does not symbolize some modern entity or nation, but represents the 10 tribes of Israel who rebelled after the death of King Solomon and formed the northern kingdom. They were conquered by and absorbed into Assyria about 720 BC. This prophecy began its fulfilment in the re-birth of Israel in 1948 and will be completed in Israel's Kingdom Age, known as the Millennium."[29]

It is more than possible that Donald Trump is from one of the ten lost tribes, known collectively as Ephraim.

Could Trump be an Antichrist and the one who prepares the way for the Antichrist or could the Jews be wrong again and Mashiach Ben Yosef morph into Mashiach Ben David or "The AntiMessiah," against their will? I believe that either of these is very possible.

---

[28] Schochet, J. Immanuel. "Appendix II." *Jewish Traditions and Mitzvah Observances*, 19 Jan. 2004, www.chabad.org/library/article_cdo/aid/101747/jewish/Appendix-II.htm.
[29] "One Messiah Or Two? – Grace thru Faith." *Grace thru Faith*, gracethrufaith.com/ask-a-bible-teacher/one-messiah-or-two/.

Time is right for the AntiMessiah…

Why Trump?

1. Trump is the one who moved the first Embassy to Jerusalem.

2. Trump is the one who first recognized Jerusalem as the Capital of Israel.

3. The Train Station in the new Embassy District was renamed the "Donald Trump Station."

4. The entire suburb where the Embassy sits is now called after Donald Trump.

5. A new shopping mall has been named after our President.

6. The Rabbis in Israel have openly identified Trump as Mashiach Ben Yosef.

7. Trump is the only individual in the world, at this moment, who has both the will and the ability to enforce a treaty which restores Israel to its full boundaries and borders as laid out in the Torah and the only one able to enforce such a treaty.

8. If this is the year 5,993 Post Adam, (or even close) we are out of time.

9. If the final fall of Damascus occurs in this year, it would be next year, at the latest, when Antichrist forces the treaty on the world.

10. Whether you think it is from God, or from the Devil, with God's permission, you *must* concede that Donald Trump has supernatural help.

I believe that Trump, if not the Antichrist himself, is indeed the one who will prepare the way for the AntiMessiah and force the seven-year treaty of Death and Hell on the world.

Even if you cannot believe that, I would most strongly encourage you to keep your mind open, keep your eyes on The Donald, and, most of all, THINK!

"Nay, Ivan," said I kindly, "I know no such word as cruelty although I do confess that right seems harsh at times, but thou wert born to serve and I to command..."

Will Donald Trump Save America?

Donald Trump is not going to rescue America because God is not going to rescue America.

Jeremiah 14:

[11] Then the Lord said to me, "Do not pray for the well-being of this people. [12] Although they fast, I will not listen to their cry; though they offer burnt offerings and grain offerings, I will not accept them. Instead, I will destroy them with the sword, famine and plague."

[13] But I said, "Alas, Sovereign Lord! The prophets keep telling them, 'You will not see the sword or suffer famine. Indeed, I will give you lasting peace in this place.'"

[14] Then the Lord said to me, "The prophets are prophesying lies in my name. I have not sent them or appointed them or spoken to them. They are prophesying to you false visions, divinations, idolatries and the delusions of their own minds. [15] Therefore this is what the Lord says about the prophets who are prophesying in my name: I did not send them, yet they are saying, 'No sword or famine will touch this land.' Those same prophets will perish by sword and famine. [16] And the people they are prophesying to will be thrown out into the streets of Jerusalem because of the famine and sword. There will be no one to bury them, their wives, their sons and their daughters. I will pour out on them the calamity they deserve. (NIV)

I hate to burst your bubble, but Americans love their sin and continue to vote for those who offer them the most freedom to sin. God has a standard. God has published his standard. America and Americans have chosen to reject that standard. God has set out exactly what a nation must do in order to avoid judgment. America has not done that and has no intention of doing so.

The American Church is in full blown apostasy. I could write five or six paragraphs here, but you already know what I would say.

As long as Americans accept Islam, Hinduism and New Age weirdness but reject Jehovah and his Son, there is not going to be any rescue. While America glorifies sodomy and insists on slaughtering a million babies a year, there is not going to be any salvation.

We are not talking saving America from the natural effects of stupid decisions. We are talking of saving America from the judgment of a God who has said, "If you do these things, I will destroy you without mercy!"

No man, heathen or saint, is going to save us from the judgment of the Holy God we have rejected, and in whose face, we continue to spit.

Mr. Trump is an interesting candidate because of the level of deception by which he has deceived the church and his appeal even to the Elect. A first rate heathen who fills his houses with statues and artwork depicting pagan gods, a prolific womanizer, a Billionaire who gained his money through theft, abuse and gambling, a solid friend of the Russian Mafia… he still garners support from Evangelicals with the simplest promises of "protecting the church" and stories about his mother's Bible. He says in two separate interviews, available on the web, that he has never repented of his sin or asked God to forgive him. He has never changed that story. He has never once testified of a personal relationship with Jesus Christ…

Be that as it may, my page is filled with comments by people who believe that he is "a baby Christian", at the least, and that he is Cyrus sent by God to save America to sin another day, at the worst. This level of delusion and deception is what makes him a prime candidate for Antichrist in my mind. More than that, he has made himself a friend of Israel and has been identified by leading Rabbis as Mashiach Ben Yosef…

JOHNNY DEPP, AND TRUMP'S BODY AS APOLLO'S HOME

"When was the last time an actor assassinated a president?" he asked a cheering crowd at the Glastonbury music festival in the U.K. on Thursday night. "Now I want to clarify, I am not an actor. I lie for a living. However, it's been awhile and maybe it's time." (Johnny Depp)[30]

How many things have been foretold in the Simpson's animated cartoon show? They predicted the attacks of 9/11 and the election of President Trump, even exact details, years in advance, riding down an escalator, and even the exact detail of his hand movements. They also have also shown Trump lying in state in a coffin.

Then there was Kathy Griffin, posing with a severed head of Donald Trump. The threats to assassinate The Donald are continuous and gaining speed. What is going on?

---

[30] "Johnny Depp: 'When Was the Last Time an Actor Assassinated a President?'." *NBCNews.com*, NBCUniversal News Group, www.nbcnews.com/pop-culture/pop-culture-news/johnny-depp-when-was-last-time-actor-assassinated-president-n775881.

KARMA

You must understand that we are dealing with Luciferians, people who have literally sold their soul to the Devil in return for wealth, fame and power. These people believe in Lucifer because they have seen him work in their lives; they have reaped the physical rewards of their devotion. One of the most basic tenants of Luciferianism is the idea of karma; *what goes around, comes around.* Luciferians believe that if they do good, it will come back to them, and if they do evil, it will come back to haunt them. What they plan to do is evil and if they did it in secret, that evil would come back on their heads.

There is a way to cheat karma however, all you must do is announce your actions in advance and give your intended victim(s) time to respond and defend themselves. If you give advance warning as the doctrine of Lucifer teaches, even though you take the action, and what you do is evil, what happens to the victim(s) is their fault, and no evil will come back on you.

These Luciferian Elitists are dead serious in what they believe. They will announce their plans, in advance, every single time. After that, what they do to us, no matter how evil, is our fault and they are protected from karma. This is why they wrote their plan to reduce the world's population to 500 million people, through the slaughter of 6.5 billion people, in granite, on the Georgia Guidestones. With that plan carved in granite and left for the world to see, they can kill as many of us as they like, with no fear of supernatural retribution.

MASONIC EGYPTION MAGIC

You must also understand that these people are pagan in the strongest sense of the word. The Elitists believe in the ancient gods and revere them. They are convinced, beyond a shadow of a doubt, that the ancient magic works, and works well. They believe they can coerce and control the demons and force them to do their bidding.

This is why America was founded with so much magic. Thirteen pieces were joined and became one… that is strong magic. Nothing is an accident.

Hold on, I am getting to the point…

The United States now represented Osiris, the brother and husband of Isis.

Washington DC, which is not legally a part of any state in the Union, represented Isis in their magic. Isis, or Washington DC, had a womb…domes in buildings have represented the womb since earliest antiquity and the Capitol Dome in Washington was the Womb of Isis.

The United States, however, was emasculated. The thirteen colonies represented each of the thirteen pieces of Osiris found by Isis… We were a complete man, missing only a phallus… Not a problem. The Egyptian Obelisk has always represented the male organ. We then built an erect phallus for Osiris… it is called the Washington Monument and it overshadows the Womb of Isis, also known as the Capitol Dome.

Interesting, both the Capital Dome and the Washington Monument, the womb of Isis and the penis of Osiris, were restored and refurbished, just in time for Trump's inauguration.

NEW WORLD ORDER

If the United States is Osiris, dead but reconstructed, and Washington DC is Isis, the dome is her womb and the monument is the penis, the child, produced in that womb will be Horus, and Horus, the son, brother and husband of Isis (Washington DC) is the New World Order or the Kingdom of the Beast.

The New World Order will be the child of Washington DC. Osiris will die, and Isis will marry the New World Order which will be both her son and her husband. (confusing isn't it?) Out of the ashes of the United States the New World Order will rise, like a Phoenix.

This is magic of the first order.

SCRIPTURE

Apollyon or Abaddon, also known as Apollo, Osiris and Nimrod, will escape from Tartarus, the Bible tells me so. But Nimrod is a spirit without a body. Antichrist must be a man and Nimrod needs a body.

"They had as their king the angel of the abyss; his name in Hebrew is Abaddon, and in Greek he has the name Apollyon." Revelation 9:11 (NASB)

NOTE: The man of sin, in 2 Thessalonians 2 Is the son of **apóleia,** (Destruction, Ruin) a form of Apollo.

TRUMP'S BODY, APOLLO'S HOME

With Johnny Depp adding his voice to the furor, it is becoming more than obvious that the Luciferian Elite are planning on killing Trump. You might be getting the idea as to why from the things you have just read, but let me spell it out for you:

It is the intention of the Elite to form a New World Order. This, in their minds, will undo the damage done by Jehovah at Babel and reunite the whole world under one government and the ancient, pagan religion of Sumer. This will be the United States of the World. What the United States was on one continent, the New World Order will be on a worldwide basis.

Apollo, who is Osiris, who is Nimrod, will be resurrected. I believe that their plan is to have Trump assassinated. His soul will go to Hell and his body will lie in state in the womb of Isis, in the shadow of the penis of Osiris. It is here, in this magical place, that the spirit of Nimrod/Osiris/Apollo will be incarnated in the body of Trump and there will be a phony resurrection. Ancient legend tells us that the face of Nimrod was deeply wounded when he was killed. The same story is found in Egyptian accounts of the death of Osiris. It is most likely that Trump will have a massive head wound.

This will be more than Egyptian magic. This will be the Devil's triumph. Lucifer never had an original thought. Everything he has ever done has been a twisted copy of something that Jehovah has done. This will be no exception. The Man of Sin will be Satan's son. Osiris was Satan's son. His mother was a Gibborum, half angel, half human, making Osiris three quarters angel, one quarter man.

"And I will put enmity Between you and the woman, And between your seed and her seed; He shall bruise you on the head, And you shall bruise him on the heel." (Genesis 3:15)

As Jesus was the Son of God, incarnate in the body of a man, Antichrist will be the seed of Satan, incarnate in the body of a man. As Jesus was killed and resurrected, so the Antichrist will be killed and resurrected. As the body of Jesus carried scars and visible wounds, the body of the Antichrist will be scarred with visible wounds.

TRUMP AS MESSIAH

I have quoted multiple articles recently, which speak of the major Rabbis in Israel speaking of Trump as one of their two Messiahs.[31] In their myth, one of their Messiahs is killed but resurrected by the other Messiah.

If Trump is killed,
- I believe that Pope Francis will be involved in the resurrection.
- There will be Marian Apparitions, both at the place, and time, of the resurrection and around the world, as Mary (Isis, Queen of Heaven) proclaims that this is her son.
- At the same time, aliens (the demons released with Apollyon) appear to help us and rescue us from ourselves.
- The Pope will call down fire from heaven and demand that the people worship the resurrected Trump.

All this is clearly spelled out plan of Lucifer. If it does not work, it is because it was not time and God thwarted their plan. I believe that it will work. I am convinced that it is time. Even the Heavens are announcing the end of time... the Tribulation is upon us...

This could be mere fantasy, but it should make you think and cause many to open their eyes...

---

[31] Berkowitz, Adam Eliyahu. "Ancient Jewish Sources Indicate Trump Will Pave Way for Third Temple: Prominent Rabbi." *Breaking Israel News | Latest News. Biblical Perspective.*, Breaking Israel News | Latest News. Biblical Perspective., 22 Mar. 2018, www.breakingisraelnews.com/104682/ancient-jewish-sources-indicate-trump-will-pave-way-for-third-temple-prominent-rabbi/.

TRUMP AND THE TREATY THAT WILL MAKE HIM GOD...

Trump is a consummate businessman. Trump knows contracts and he knows how to leverage people and make them sign contracts; contracts that are often to their detriment. A treaty is nothing more than a glorified contract; a contract between nations. Trump will be a master Treaty Maker and nations will sign treaties that place their own nations at a disadvantage. Trump knows how to do that, and all the powers of Hell stand by to give him whatever assistance he needs.

The fall of Babylon, described in Revelation 18, follows the seventh Bowl Judgment in Revelation 16. This is not at the beginning, but at the end, of the Tribulation. I have described, in other places, why I believe that the United States is the Babylon of Revelation.

I used to believe that Babylon, America, would fall at the beginning of the Tribulation, however, I now believe that it falls very near the end. The fact that it follows the seventh Bowl Judgment and that John was shown the fall by one of the angels holding the bowls makes that scenario quite logical.

IMAGINE:

Let us imagine that America does not die, per se, in order that the New World Order / Kingdom of the Beast can rise. Let us imagine instead, that America is the foundation and the seat of power for the New World Order and the Kingdom of the Beast. Let us imagine that the "Spirit of America" is rebirthed under Trump's leadership and that that system goes worldwide; Life, Liberty and the Pursuit of Happiness becomes the rallying cry of the Beast...

Let's say that this spirit of universal freedom and happiness overtakes the world and that, under one world government, seated in New York or Washington, the values of the New Atlantis become the values of most of the world. There will be pockets of resistance of course, and we will fight wars to enforce freedom and happiness around the world. Islam will be defeated, and the remnant will retreat to desert caves.

Babylonian Christians, those who have mistaken America for the Kingdom of God and the light of Lucifer for the Glory of God, will cheer! God is winning, and Trump has brought us freedom, money, and success, and he has killed all those awful Muslims! Praise God!

A cowered and battered Palestinian Authority will be ready to sign anything, and Donald Trump will have the perfect Treaty:

- The Palestinians will get a limited State.
- The Jews will get their Temple
- The Vatican will get sovereignty over Jerusalem and enforce the peace with United Nations Troops.

What a deal! Everybody gets what they want. Israel expands its borders to unprecedented size and there is peace in Israel... The whole world is adopting American values, Freedom is in the air and religions, once the seat of great division and turmoil, are now uniting under Pope Francis... The Televangelists and the Babylonian Christians are thrilled out of their minds... Rick Warren is in Seventh Heaven and Kenneth Copeland is made a Bishop in the Church of Rome... Even the Muslims are coming onboard... Hindus and Buddhists are thrilled... Pagan religions, from the smallest to the largest are falling under the spell of Pope Francis and embracing *Life. Liberty, the Pursuit of Happiness* and Donald Trump! It is a wonderful world!

But peace comes with a price. A simple pledge *and* a *tiny microchip*... Starvation and death hits the Bible Believers hard.

For three and a half years the Jews work on their Temple. Donald Trump is spending an inordinate amount of time in Israel. He is Israel's greatest friend and loudest cheerleader!

The Priests are put in place and the daily sacrifice is resumed for the first time in two thousand years! Israel holds a ceremony and declares Donald Trump is the Messiah!

And Christians... even the Babylonian variety, begin to rebel...

For three years or more, the cry has rung out around the world...
"DOCTRINE BE DAMNED... UNITY AT ANY COST!"

- Suddenly, even the Babylonian Christians can no longer stomach the situation. There is a great revival... not so much of numbers as in a return to holiness...
- Pope Francis and The Donald are not amused. The fate that fell on Muslims in the early days, now falls on Christians.
- Then comes the Temple Dedication. The Donald, now known in Israel as The Messiah, will preside...

- Then comes the revelation of the Statue in a wing of the Temple and the Jews are appalled…
- Then comes the "I am God" speech.
- Then comes…all Hell breaks loose…

Just imagine….

Put Mr. Trump down as my choice for the Antichrist, or a "John the Baptist" who prepares the way for the Antichrist.

HEGEL

I found myself caught up in the morning news today. I caught my emotions flaring as something in me rose up in defense of President Trump. And then, I laughed.

I know that in Babylon, the show government does not rule. I know that all is a well scripted Soap Opera, a "Made for Television" production. Still, just as I can get caught up in the emotions of any well-made movie. I can get caught up with the Illuminati Television Production, called "*GOVERNMENT*".

What bothers me is that, if I, knowing all that I know, can get caught up, what chance does the average Christian have of seeing through the charade? No one in church is educating them on these things. Chances are that their Pastors are as ignorant, or more so, than they. I would venture to guess that the majority of Christian Pastors in America believe everything they see on CNN Television.

I want to take the opportunity to tell you, or remind you, of the truth today; neither Trump nor the White House, nor the Congress rule in America. More binding decisions are made at the George Washington Lodge in Washington DC than will ever be made in Congress. It is the Rothschilds, and the Luciferian Elite who make phone calls, on behalf of Lucifer, and run the government.

The very public fight you watch on your television is a distraction, leading to a crisis. Soon the crisis will threaten the peace and security of every American. When we are all duly frightened, they will offer us a solution. We will have to give up a few more freedoms, of course, but in return, the government will guarantee our peace and security. This is the Hegelian Dialectic, and the Hegelian Dialectic was in full force this morning on NBC.

I have done this so that we may not be taken advantage of by Satan. For we are not ignorant of his schemes.´ 2 Corinthians 2:11

Unfortunately, most of the Pastors and churches in America are totally and completely unaware of Satan's schemes.

Please! Today, right now, stop and think. Open your eyes. Your Pastor may take his church to Hell, but you do not have to go along for the ride.

OUR COMING CIVIL WAR

I see war. I see a terrible, destructive civil war. I see at least a third of all Americans dying in a war that pits race against race, religion against religion and conservative against liberal.

I believe that Donald Trump will invoke Martial Law. I see Obama rising up against him. I see two Presidents competing with the people, and the police and the military all dividing up; some siding with Trump, others standing with Obama.

I see David Wilkerson's vision of New York burning[32] and how it fits in with the biblical account of Babylon burning. I see the New World Order rising out of the ashes like a phoenix.

Real or imagined, the pagans, occultists, and the secret societies, see a war, not between Satan and the God of Heaven, but a war between Satan, the current god of this world and Lucifer, the coming king. Satan is black, dark and evil. Satan hates men and seeks to destroy them. Lucifer is a bright and shining light whom they believe seeks to enlighten men and lift them up so that they may become as gods.

I suspect that Satan and Lucifer are two sides of the same fallen angel. Scripture tells us that, *"even Satan can appear as an angel of light." (2 Corinthians 11:14)*

Obama is Satan and the Christians hate him.

Trump is Lucifer and the carnal, blind Christians embrace him.

The carnal and the blind, easily mistake the light of Lucifer for the Glory of a God they have never known...

Did you know that when Barack Obama won the Presidential election, Donald Trump was one of the first to tweet his congratulations, "To my friend?"

---

[32] Challenge, World. "AN URGENT MESSAGE." *English - World Challenge Devotions Blog*, Blogger, 7 Mar. 2009, davidwilkersontoday.blogspot.com/2009/03/urgent-message.html.

Trump and Obama, like Lucifer and Satan, are one and the same. It is a game in which one appears as dark and the other as light. It is as dark and light that they will lead the nation into war and destruction. It is out of a game of good and evil that destruction comes.

It is out of destruction that the New World Order is to be born. It is out of the smoke and the fire that Antichrist will rise.

This is not a prophecy. This is my vision of the future. If it happens, understand what is happening.

Be wise...

THE MAN OF LAWLESSNESS IS REVEALED

The carnal and the blind, easily mistake the light of Lucifer, for the Glory of God they have never known...

2 Thessalonians 2

The Man of Lawlessness

1 Now concerning the

COMING OF OUR LORD JESUS CHRIST and OUR BEING GATHERED TO HIM:

We ask you, brothers, 2 not to be easily upset in mind or troubled, either by a spirit or by a message or by a letter as if from us, alleging that the Day of the Lord has come.

3 DON'T LET ANYONE DECEIVE YOU in any way.

For THAT DAY WILL NOT COME UNLESS

THE APOSTASY COMES FIRST and

THE MAN OF LAWLESSNESS IS REVEALED,

the son of destruction. 4 He opposes and exalts himself above every so-called god or object of worship, so that he sits in God's sanctuary, publicizing that he himself is God.

CONCERNING:

THE COMING OF OUR LORD JESUS CHRIST

OUR BEING GATHERED TO HIM:

DON'T LET ANYONE DECEIVE YOU!

THAT DAY WILL NOT COME

UNLESS

THE APOSTASY COMES FIRST
THE MAN OF LAWLESSNESS IS REVEALED.

THE APOSTASY IS ALL AROUND US. If you are saved, you cannot help but see it.

THE FALSE PROPHET WAS REVEALED on September 25, 2015 at the United Nations.

THE BEAST IS YET TO COME.

NIMROD WILL RISE…

Can you see what this means?
Do you follow?
Are your spiritual ears open?
Can you hear what the Spirit is saying to the Church?

LUCIFER AS GOD
The Quest Fulfilled

"We shall unleash the nihilists and the atheists and we shall provoke a great social cataclysm which in all its horror will show clearly to all nations the effect of absolute atheism; the origins of savagery and of most bloody turmoil.

Then everywhere, the people will be forced to defend themselves against the world minority of the world revolutionaries and will exterminate those destroyers of civilization and the multitudes disillusioned with Christianity whose spirits will be from that moment without direction and leadership and anxious for an ideal, but without knowledge where to send its adoration, will receive the true light through the universal manifestation of the pure doctrine of Lucifer brought finally out into public view. A manifestation which will result from a general reactionary movement which will follow the destruction of Christianity and Atheism; both conquered and exterminated at the same time."[33]

Let me lay a foundation: In 1978, Iran was Israel's strongest ally in the Middle East. Wealthy Israelis vacationed on Turkey's beautiful beaches and Ezekiel 38 made no sense at all. Recently, Putin met with Erdoğan of Turkey and Iran's Rouhani in Moscow and the stage is set for the war described by the Prophet. Ezekiel saw Turkey, Iran, and

---

[33] "A Quote by Albert Pike." *Goodreads*, Goodreads, www.goodreads.com/quotes/1286683-we-shall-unleash-the-nihilists-and-the-atheists-and-we.

Russia, all together, in an all-out assault against Israel. There are Biblical, and secular, hints that China will march down, crossing the dried-up Euphrates to attack Israel as well. They all attack through Syria. Surprise, surprise, surprise…

Ezekiel 38:3 This is what the Lord God says: Look, I am against you, Gog, chief prince of Meshach and Tubal. (Russia) 4 I will turn you around, put hooks in your jaws, and bring you out with all your army, including horses and riders, who are all splendidly dressed, a huge company armed with shields and bucklers, all of them brandishing swords. 5 Persia, Cush, and Put are with them… (HCSB)

Israel is now known to have the largest supply of oil of any nation in the world. *This reserve dwarfs Saudi Arabia and Russia combined.*[34] God says that He will put a hook in Russia's mouth and drag her down, with her entire military, to attack Israel. She will be joined by Iran, Turkey and Syria. The U.S. and Saudi Arabia may sit it out, talking but doing nothing. Then again, it could be Trump's sign to start playing Messiah. Oil is the hook that God is using.

Damascus is the oldest continually occupied city in the world. Strangely enough, one of the Biblical signs of the End-Times is the destruction of Damascus. The Israeli oil field stretches north from the Golan and finds its northern border under the streets of Damascus… That just might explain the annihilation of that once beautiful city.

Ezekiel says that it is God himself who is pulling Russia down to attack Israel. He also says that God is going to use that opportunity to destroy Russia. God says that He will cause a massive, mountain leveling earthquake in Israel and that he will rain fire and hail from the

---

[34] "Oil in the North: Moses' Blessing Coming to Life." *The Jerusalem Post | JPost.com*, 27 Feb. 2018, www.jpost.com/Christian-News/Oil-in-the-North-Moses-blessing-coming-to-life-543719.

skies, obliterating the attacking armies. God says that it will be so violent that the world will, for a moment, recognize it as his doing.

This will, at the same time, destroy the old centers of both Islam and Atheism. The head of the Caliphate and the heads of the world's communist empires both destroyed with a single blow. Neither will ever recover. This will leave the Vatican, Pope Francis and the Roman Catholic Church as the undisputed power center of the world.

The Israeli oil field stretches north from the Golan and finds its northern border under the streets of Damascus...

Ancient Map of Damascus

You must understand three things at this point:

1. The Roman Catholic Church is and always has been the center of ancient Pagan Religion in the West. It is not, and never has been a Christian Church. They baptized the ancient gods, giving them Christian names, and mixed in some Christian words, but the doctrine and dogma of the church lines up with the ancient worship of Osiris, Isis, Horus, Apollo and the rest, not the Bible or the God of the Bible.

2. The United States is the Daughter of Rome, something a quick tour of Washington DC will quickly substantiate.

3. The Masonic Lodge in Washington DC is the repository of Jesuit Mysticism and ancient occultic religion on the American Continent... The official name of the building is a mind bender: *"The Supreme Council (Mother Council of the World) of the Inspectors General Knights Commander of the House of the Temple of Solomon of the Thirty-third degree of the Ancient and Accepted Scottish Rite of Freemasonry of the Southern Jurisdiction of the United States of America."* (Yes, *every* word of that is the name.)

That Temple contains a museum devoted to Albert Pike, who rewrote the Scottish Rite rituals and headed its Supreme Council from 1859 until his death in 1891, and whose remains are buried in the House of the Temple.

Albert Pike wrote about the Third World war. Three points stand out in that dissertation.

1. The war must be conducted in such a way that Islam (the Moslem Arabic World) and political Zionism (the State of Israel) mutually destroy each other.
2. Will show clearly to the nations the effect of absolute atheism, origin of savagery and of the most bloody turmoil.
3. The multitude, disillusioned with Christianity… will receive the true light through the universal manifestation of the pure doctrine of Lucifer, brought finally out in the public view.
4. This manifestation will result from the general reactionary movement which will follow the destruction of Christianity and atheism, both conquered and exterminated at the same time.[35]

Lest you laugh at that scenario, may I point out that his predictions for World Wars One and Two, were letter perfect and both wars happened *exactly* as predicted.

And he was permitted to wage war against the saints and to conquer them. He was also given authority over every tribe, people, language, and nation. Revelation 13:7 (HCSB)

It is the godless and atheistic Left; the socialists and communists who have destroyed the world. Most understand that fact.

The Muslims are hated and feared because of their bent towards terrorism and mass murder.

The World hates the Jews and Israel because of the God of Abraham, whom they reject outright.

The Christians are the most hated of all because their very presence convicts the world of sin and righteousness and judgment.

---

[35] "A Quote by Albert Pike." *Goodreads*, Goodreads, www.goodreads.com/quotes/1286683-we-shall-unleash-the-nihilists-and-the-atheists-and-we.

It is the goal of Lucifer and the Luciferian elite to pit all of these groups against each other, resulting in the mutual destruction of all and the much-coveted reduction in the world's population.

The next section is inserted with the goal of convincing you that the people preaching population reduction are dead serious...

POPULATION REDUCTION

The following are 30 population control quotes which show that the elite truly believe that humans are a plague upon the earth and that a great culling is necessary.[36]

1. *"We are a plague on the Earth. It's coming home to roost over the next 50 years or so. It's not just climate change; it's sheer space, places to grow food for this enormous horde. Either we limit our population growth, or the natural world will do it for us, and the natural world is doing it for us right now."* UK Television Presenter Sir David Attenborough

2. *"To our minds, the fundamental cure, reducing the scale of the human enterprise (including the size of the population) to keep its aggregate consumption within the carrying capacity of Earth is obvious but too much neglected or denied."* Paul Ehrlich, a former science adviser to president George W. Bush and the author of "The Population Bomb"

---

[36] Snyder, Michael. "Michael Snyder." *The Truth*, 23 June 2015, thetruthwins.com/archives/30-population-control-quotes-that-show-that-the-elite-truly-believe-that-humans-are-a-plague-upon-the-earth.

3., *"Nobody, in my view, has the right to have 12 children or even three unless the second pregnancy is twins."* Paul Ehrlich.

4. *"We humans have become a disease, the Humanpox."* Dave Foreman, the co-founder of Earth First.

5. *"A total world population of 250-300 million people, a 95% decline from present levels, would be ideal."* CNN Founder Ted Turner

6. About medical patients with serious illnesses: *"You cannot sleep well when you think it's all paid by the government. This won't be solved unless you let them hurry up and die."* Japan's Deputy Prime Minister Taro Aso

7. *'The negative impact of population growth on all of our planetary ecosystems is becoming appallingly evident."* David Rockefeller

8. *"On a finite planet, the optimum population providing the best quality of life for all, is clearly much smaller than the maximum, permitting bare survival. The more we are, the less for each; fewer people mean better lives."* Environmental activist Roger Martin

9. *"I'm pro-choice, I'm for assisted suicide, I'm for regular suicide, I'm for whatever gets the freeway moving – that's what I'm for. It's too crowded, the planet is too crowded, and we need to promote death."* HBO personality Bill Maher

10. *"The real trick is, in terms of trying to level off at someplace lower than that 9 billion, is to get the birthrates in the developing countries to drop as fast as we can. And that will determine the level at which humans will level off on earth."* MIT professor Penny Chisholm

11. *"The only known solution to ecological overshoot is to decelerate our population growth faster than it's decelerating now and eventually reverse it—at the same time we slow and eventually reverse the rate at which we consume the planet's resources. Success in these twin endeavors will crack our most pressing global issues: climate change, food scarcity, water supplies, immigration, health care, biodiversity loss, even war. On one front, we've already made unprecedented strides, reducing global fertility from an average 4.92 children per woman in 1950 to 2.56 today—an accomplishment of trial and sometimes brutally coercive error, but also a result of one woman at a time making her individual choices. The speed of this childbearing revolution, swimming hard against biological programming, rates as perhaps our greatest collective feat to date."* Julia Whitty, a columnist for Mother Jones

12. *"Ending human population growth is almost certainly a necessary (but not sufficient) condition for preventing catastrophic global climate change. Indeed, significantly reducing current human numbers may be necessary in order to do so."* Colorado State University Professor Philip Cafaro in a paper entitled "Climate Ethics and Population Policy"

13. *"I do not bear any ill will toward people. However, I am convinced that the world, including all humanity, WOULD clearly be much better off without so many of us."* Professor of Biology at the University of Texas at Austin Eric R. Pianka

14. *"Since the national attention is on birth control, here's my idea: If we want to fight poverty, reduce violent crime and bring down our embarrassing drop-out rate, we should swap contraceptives for fluoride*

in Michigan's drinking water....We've got a baby problem in Michigan. Too many babies are born to immature parents who don't have the skills to raise them, too many are delivered by poor women who can't afford them, and too many are fathered by sorry layabouts who spread their seed like dandelions and then wander away from the consequences." Detroit News Columnist Nolan Finley

15 *"The effect on the planet of having one child less is an order of magnitude greater than all these other things we might do, such as switching off lights. An extra child is the equivalent of a lot of flights across the planet."* John Guillebaud, professor of family planning at University College London

16. *"WE need death panels. Well, maybe not death panels, exactly, but unless we start allocating health care resources more prudently — rationing, by its proper name — the exploding cost of Medicare will swamp the federal budget."* Democrat strategist Steven Rattner

17. *"But not only is this health care spending on the elderly the key issue in the federal budget, our disproportionate allocation of health care dollars to old people surely accounts for the remarkable lack of apparent cost effectiveness of the American health care system. When the patient is already over 80, the simple fact of the matter is that no amount of treatment is going to work miracles in terms of life expectancy or quality of life."* Matthew Yglesias, a business and economics correspondent for Slate, in an article entitled "The Case for Death Panels, in One Chart"

18. *"All of our problems are the result of overbreeding among the working class."* Planned Parenthood Founder Margaret Sanger

19. *"Frankly I had thought that at the time Roe was decided, there was concern about population growth and particularly growth in populations that we don't want to have too many of."* U.S. Supreme Court Justice Ruth Bader Ginsburg

20. *"The most merciful thing that the large family does to one of its infant members is to kill it."* Planned Parenthood Founder Margaret Sanger

21. *"All life is not equal. That's a difficult thing for liberals like me to talk about, lest we wind up looking like death-panel-loving, kill-your-grandma-and-your-precious-baby storm troopers. Yet a fetus can be a human life without having the same rights as the woman in whose body it resides."* Salon columnist Mary Elizabeth Williams in an article entitled "So What If Abortion Ends Life?"

22. *"[W]hen circumstances occur after birth such that they would have justified abortion, what we call after-birth abortion should be permissible. ... [W]e propose to call this practice 'after-birth abortion', rather than 'infanticide,' to emphasize that the moral status of the individual killed is comparable with that of a fetus ... rather than to that of a child. Therefore, we claim that killing a newborn could be ethically permissible in all the circumstances where abortion would be. Such circumstances include cases where the newborn has the potential to have an (at least) acceptable life, but the well-being of the family is at risk."* Alberto Giubilini of Monash University in Melbourne, Australia and Francesca Minerva of the University of Melbourne in a paper published in the Journal of Medical Ethics

23. *"We need to continue to decrease the growth rate of the global population; the planet can't support many more people."* Nina Fedoroff, a key adviser to Hillary Clinton

24. *"A program of sterilizing women after their second or third child, despite the relatively greater difficulty of the operation than vasectomy, might be easier to implement than trying to sterilize men...The development of a long-term sterilizing capsule that could be implanted under the skin and removed when pregnancy is desired opens additional possibilities for coercive fertility control. The capsule could be implanted at puberty and might be removable, with official permission, for a limited number of births."* Barack Obama's primary science adviser, John P. Holdren

25. *"Childbearing [should be] a punishable crime against society, unless the parents hold a government license ... All potential parents [should be] required to use contraceptive chemicals, the government issuing antidotes to citizens chosen for childbearing."* David Brower, the first Executive Director of the Sierra Club:

26. *"There is a single theme behind all our work–we must reduce population levels. Either governments do it our way, through nice clean methods, or they will get the kinds of mess that we have in El Salvador, or in Iran or in Beirut. Population is a political problem. Once population is out of control, it requires authoritarian government, even fascism, to reduce it..."* Thomas Ferguson, former official in the U.S. State Department Office of Population Affairs

27. *"We must speak more clearly about sexuality, contraception, about abortion, about values that control population, because the ecological crisis, in short, is the population crisis. Cut the population*

by 90% and there aren't enough people left to do a great deal of ecological damage." Mikhail Gorbachev

28. *"In order to stabilize world population, we must eliminate 350,000 people per day. It is a horrible thing to say, but it is just as bad not to say it."* Jacques Costeau

29. *"If there were a button I could press, I would sacrifice myself without hesitating if it meant millions of people would die."* Finnish environmentalist Pentti Linkola

30. *"In the event that I am reincarnated, I would like to return as a deadly virus, in order to contribute something to solve overpopulation."* Prince Phillip, husband of Queen Elizabeth II and co-founder of the World Wildlife Fund

So, what is left after the war, if Christians, Jews, Muslims and Atheists are all destroyed? The world is left with a One World Government, a single world ruler, a Luciferian Elite, and a greatly reduced population; demonized, convinced worshipers of Lucifer and the old gods. Useful surfs who will serve and provide for the Elite Class.

The day that Russia, Turkey, and Iran, march through Syria and into the Golan is fast approaching... That, according to both the Bible and the Luciferians, will lead to WWIII, followed by a false peace under the Antichrist.

You will note that this scenario contradicts those shared in other chapters. I would remind you that, apart from Scripture quoted, nothing in this volume is given as if it were an infallible Word from God. This author has studied widely, prayed profusely, and thought deeply, on these things. The future described here is the result of much prayer and study.

The purpose of this book remains the same: *to cause Christians to think...*

As I write this, I am still leaning towards a Right-Wing World Order as the most likely outcome of current events. I still look for a Luciferian, Talmudic Jew of the line and lineage of David to take his place in the Temple and proclaim himself God.

One way or the other, Nimrod shall reign and Lucifer shall be crowned God of this World.

WASHINGTON DC SYMBOLISM AND MASONIC CONNECTIONS

In Europe, occult leaders were told by their familiar spirits as early as the 1740's, that the new American continent was to be established as the new Atlantis and its destiny was to assume the global leadership of the drive to the New World Order. The United States of America was chosen to lead the world into this kingdom of Antichrist from the very beginning. This is evidenced by the preponderance of occult symbols in Washington DC.

The boundaries of the city, established by George Washington in 1791 form a square ten miles long on each side, cantered on the originally proposed location for the Washington Monument. The east-west diagonal of the square crosses over the Capitol building and the north-south crosses over the White House. George Washington, a Master Mason, selected French designer Pierre Charles L'Enfant to design the city's layout in Washington DC

The mall in Washington DC is laid out so the gardens and streets form the image of an owl. The owl is representative of the mythical goddess, Lilirh.

The street design in Washington, DC has been laid out in such a manner that certain Luciferic symbols are depicted by the streets, cul-de-sacs and rotaries. This design was created in 1791, a few years after Freemasonry assumed the leadership of the new World Order, in 1782.

The first series of symbols deal with the Executive Branch of government, the White House, indicated by arrow. If you are a google earther you can see these satellite images for yourself at Google Maps. The White House sits at the apex of an inverted pentagram. This symbol is incomplete by only two small pieces.

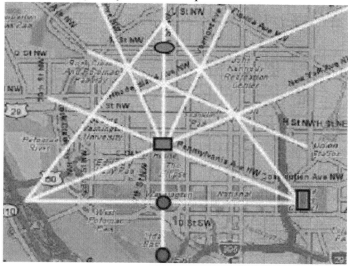

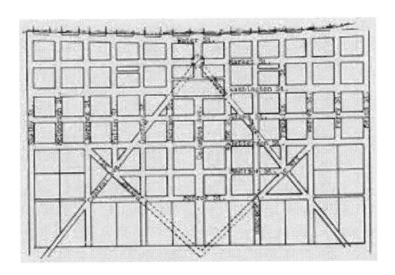

Where is the seeing eye, the exact address? House of the Temple, masonic lodge headquarters Washington DC. Designed in replication of the Tomb of Mansolus.

A BRUTALLY HONEST RANT

Thus, Antichrist will be dead and resurrected. He will be
Satan and he will be the son of Satan, incarnate in the body
of a man…

We are out of time. Does that statement grab you? It is the truth… we are the last generation. God is giving us so many signs and the Elect can see it and feel it.

I watched an Alex Jones clip concerning the soon coming assassination of Donald Trump. (That clip has been removed from YouTube since they changed the Constitution and restricted free speech.) He played the clip from Rodney Howard Brown where he speaks of his conversation with an unnamed Senator who spoke openly of that assassination and called it unavoidable. He showed those

Televangelists surrounding Trump. Trump has a look of bewilderment on his face...

Satan often calls himself "Jesus"; he appears "as an angel of light."

Jesus said, "Deny yourself, take up your cross and follow me."

Satan said, "If you will bow down to me, I will give you all these things."

That is a good standard by which to judge...

When you hear people preaching, you must ask yourself...

"Which Jesus is he/she/it preaching?"

Pardon me, but I think that those Televangelists who prayed for Trump, preach another Jesus...

For many reasons, reasons, reasons which I have written on both here and on Facebook, *I believe that this assassination is going to be used to provide Apollyon with a body.* (Research that) Things are going to get supernatural and they are going to get supernatural fast.

This is a rant, not a theological thesis, but all the reasons for what I am saying have been discussed, at length on my blog and a million other places... *Do your homework...*

Scripture speaks to Satan being cast to the earth and of Apollyon rising. Apollyon is Nimrod, is Gilgamesh, is Osiris/Horus, is Apollo, is Abaddon... One guy with many names. He was the bad guy at the fall of Babel.

His Spirit/soul has been confined in Tartarus since the death of his body. He is, *by legend,* three quarters fallen angel and one quarter human. He is Nephilim. He has no body, but he will rule the world. He is of the seven and the eighth world ruler, the first and the last, he who was, is not, and is to come.... Satan's Antichrist.

I believe that he will be much like Jesus, in a bad way. *Satan only copies and twists... he will do nothing new.* Antichrist will be the first and the last (world ruler). He will appear to be dead and resurrected. As Jesus has visible wounds, so the Antichrist will have visible wounds, mortal wounds.

This is what I believe is being set up now with the well planned and publicized assassination of Trump.

The Capitol Dome is the "Womb of Isis" (Where Horus is born as Osiris reincarnated) The Washington Monument is the Phallus of Osiris... There is a pagan goddess mounted on top of the dome and the inside is covered with The Apotheosis of Washington, where he is shown, as God, on a throne, surrounded by pagan gods and goddesses. This has been planned for centuries.

When Trump is assassinated, his body will lie in state, in the Womb of Isis, for three days. If Satan can pull it off, and I believe that this is his time, Apollyon will escape, without a body. Trump will be in Hell, his body in the womb of Isis.

I shared earlier, all the reasons that I believe that Pope Francis is the False Prophet. I believe he will come for Trump's funeral. This has nothing to do with whether they like each other or not...

What I believe will happen then is that the Pontiff will pray, and Apollyon will enter the dead body of Trump and animate it. There, in the Womb of Isis, Antichrist will be born... and the whole world will marvel and follow after the Beast.

I would fully expect a Marian Apparition (Isis) to appear at the time and declare to the world,

"This is my Beloved Son, in whom I am well pleased."

Thus, Antichrist will be dead and resurrected. He will be Satan and he will be the son of Satan, incarnate in the body of a man...

Every preacher of that other Jesus, will pronounce this as a true miracle from God and demand that Christians everywhere follow Trump and Pope Francis...

"Obviously," they will shout, "this is none other than Jesus Christ returned to lead the world..." Millions and millions of "Christians" will believe them and swear their allegiance.

I can see this as if it happened yesterday and was on the News all day today...

Could this just be my imagination? Of course.

Even if I am wrong, wouldn't this be a great time to get right with Jesus?

THE DEATH OF THE REPUBLIC

Let us not forget the Devil's Quest. Since God has told us that the New World Order will arise, and since God has very clearly given signs that tell us that this event is imminent, it seems foolish, to me, for a Christian to spend a great deal of time defending the Republic.

Why would you save that which God has told you is going to die?

If your hope is in America, you are much to be pitied...

CARAVAN

Perhaps it will turn out to be nothing. Perhaps, by the time you read this, the world will have forgotten, but today, thousands of Central Americans are in Mexico. They form a large caravan, determined to cross the border into the Disney World they have been told is the United States. I have lived in the Third World and I will tell you that their picture of the USA much more resembles Disney Land than it does any place that you might know. If they can only get across that border, they will all have jobs and cars and servants and houses and gardens and they, unlike their Uncle who never sent anything, will be able to send hundreds of Dollars to their relatives back home... perhaps they can support their whole village. Imagine that! They have a dream!!

The people who organized and financed the migrant caravan have a different dream. They would use these poor people and their dream to weaken the border and allow unlimited immigration into America, in effect, killing the land of dreams.

Make no mistake, the leaders have no intention of fulfilling the dreams of these people. They would prefer to turn America into a clone of Honduras or Guatemala. They are set on destroying America.

One of the quickest ways of killing America is to fill it with people who have no education, no money, no skills, and no attachment to America. These people have not come in order to become Americans. They have come to use America to fulfil *their* dreams and enrichen their families back home. Those who finance and bring them here want the migrant votes (and they know that they will vote the way they are told!) If enough of migrants come, they can vote the Republic out of existence.

The Military is going to stand down to the migrant caravan invasion. If one soldier was to be shot, the retaliation would be terrible. The hope is to create such horror that it leads to the death of America.

One incident could do it. Whatever happens will weaken the Republic and help to lead the Nation to destruction.

Why would they destroy America?

We must go back to our original premise. Satan is working to undo Babel. America came as close as any nation on earth to fulfilling Satan's quest. But the rest of the world is not impressed. No nation on earth is going to lay down its flag and raise the American flag. The entire world is not going to surrender to America.

If America dies, the American dream can be sold to the world. Why only rebuild America? Rebuild the world! Form one government! The United States can join with the whole world and submit to the new flag and the new government! Let Honduras, Nicaragua, Guatemala, Europe, Africa, and Asia all join together!

If more than half the residents of the United States fail to identify as Americans, why not? What do they care if America takes down her flag?

Where do we go from here?

There are two scenarios I think Lucifer would be happy with:
1. Civil War
2. A Right-wing paradise

Civil War: This time, it will not be north against South or even one side against the other. There will be hundreds of splinter groups, all committed to killing everybody else. The Muslims will start killing anyone who will not convert. Blacks will start killing Whites and whites will split, some killing blacks, others killing whites who are killing blacks. Latinos will kill anybody who doesn't speak Spanish. Democrats will kill Republicans and Republicans will kill Democrats. The Government in Washington will kill anybody who doesn't work for the Government. Republican officers will lead attacks on Democratic Officers. Soldiers will desert in order to join militias with whom they agree. As for me, I am going to start Street Preaching. When it is over, the survivors will raise any flag you hand them.

Right-wing Paradise: This scenario has Trump declaring Martial Law with military in agreement with him. All the bad guys are rounded up and executed. Survivors change their party affiliation to Republican. Business prospers, and there is money everywhere. The televangelists start praying to Trump. America attacks all the enemies of Israel and destroy them All the other nations bow down to America. People around the world hail Trump as Savior and Lord. The Dominionists and the Seven Mountaineers all declare Trump as Messiah and the one who is preparing the way for the return of Christ.

Trump declares a One World Government and moves it to Israel. In Israel, he builds a Temple…

Take your pick…

Whatever happens, America dies, the New World Order rises, the AntiMessiah makes war against the Saints and conquers them…The bad news is, Jesus said, *"He who endures to the end will be saved…"*

Personally, I don't like the enduring part. I would prefer to have been born in 1938 and die an old man, tomorrow, before all this goes down. But God put me in the here and now. The days ahead are going to be Hell on earth for those of us who insist on following the Jesus of the Bible. But great is your reward in Heaven. I would love to end with a happy word...

This is my final word:

HE WHO ENDURES TO THE END SHALL BE SAVED.

EPILOGUE

THE NEW WORLD ORDER: America On Steroids!
"Thus, the struggle for peace includes the struggle for freedom and justice for the masses of all countries…"
(Arthur Henderson, British Politician)[37]

I just keep thinking, Trump is going to keep winning and the NWO is going to be a Rightwing, American style government. Why would the NWO not promote the values of the American Patriarchs on a worldwide scale? Why would they not sell freedom and justice for all to the whole world? Why would they not rescue us from the communists, the Muslims, the violent Hindus, the Bible Believing Christians and others who seek to divide?

I am thinking that, as America dies, a bigger and better monster will arise. America has been a rousing success; the most successful nation the world has ever seen. America has outdone them all. Communism has never worked. The Elite know that. If you want to see how well Islam works, look at the millions of Muslims fleeing the nations their religion has ruined. How well does Hinduism work? Walk the streets of New Deli for an hour and you will know. No, it is *American Democracy* that has worked the very best. Even the Devil likes what works.

---

[37] "Arthur Henderson Quotes." *BrainyQuote*, Xplore,
www.brainyquote.com/quotes/arthur_henderson_199070.

Nothing has ever succeeded in undoing Babel and reuniting people once divided by tribe, tongue and nation, like America.

You must remember that, apart from the cross, the greatest victory Jehovah ever won against Lucifer was the division of mankind at Babel. Lucifer was winning in Babel. It is the division of mankind that has frustrated him ever since, and it is the *undoing of Babel* that is the number one goal of Hell. Godless communism did not work. False Religion has not worked. American Democracy *works*.

I must ask:

- If it worked on a continent, why not expand it to the world?
- What if a hero rode in on a white horse and rescued the world from itself?
- What if he freed people in bondage to communism, tyrants and religions?
- What if he promoted unity and freedom?
- What if he insisted that all men are created equal?
- What if he succeeded in removing the barriers that divide us? What if he made great speeches declaring that all men have been endowed by their Creator with certain inalienable rights?
- What if he so inspired both Jew and Arab that they laid down their arms and made a real peace treaty work?
- What if he came up with a new and novel idea that gave the Palestinians a homeland that did not divide Israel?
- What if he helped the Jews build their Temple?

What would happen if the only thing demanded was a loyalty oath that thrilled the apostate church but horrified those who know their Bible?

What if he allowed you to be a Christian or a Muslim or a Jew or a Hindu… just like you have always been, but you must give your first loyalty to the state and agree to do nothing, in any way, that would interfere with another religion? What if you could be a Christian but you could never claim that your religion had the truth or that it was in any way superior to anyone else's religion and you could never try to convert anyone to your religion?

What if they believed so strongly in Freedom of Religion that proselytism, in any form, was a death penalty offense?

What if the only rule was that you could never discuss your religion outside of your home or your church, Mosque or Temple? You could believe in Jesus any way you please, but you could never interfere with another's right to believe what they believe?

The United States of America has been the most successful experiment in undoing Babel and reuniting the world under Lucifer that has ever occurred.

I would not be surprised to see this great Puppet Show end with a great surprise; with all the forces of Hell seeming aligned against it, Babylon rises victorious and wins the world with a promise of Freedom and Justice for All!

David

BIBLIOGRAPHY

Golden Screen Cinemas, ipfs.io/ipfs/QmXoypizjW3WknFiJnKLwHCnL72vedxjQkDDP1mXW o6uco/wiki/Annuit_coeptis.html.

The Gnostic Jesus - Adam and Eve, www.gnostic-jesus.com/gnostic-jesus/Overview/adam-and-eve.html.

Virginia-Maryland Boundary for Chesapeake Bay/Eastern Shore, www.virginiaplaces.org/boundaries/wvboundary.html.

[Pike, Albert]. *Morals and Dogma of the Ancient and Accepted Scottish Rite of Freemasonry: Prepared for the Supreme Council of the Thirty-Third Degree for the Southern Jurisdiction of the United States and Published by Its Authority.: Esoteric Book, for Scottish Rite Use Only; to Be Returned upon Withdrawal of Death of Recipient.* 1950.

"A Quote by Albert Pike." *Goodreads,* Goodreads, www.goodreads.com/quotes/1286683-we-shall-unleash-the-nihilists-and-the-atheists-and-we.

"A Quote by Albert Pike." *Goodreads,* Goodreads, www.goodreads.com/quotes/1286683-we-shall-unleash-the-nihilists-and-the-atheists-and-we.

"Arthur Henderson Quotes." *BrainyQuote,* Xplore, www.brainyquote.com/quotes/arthur_henderson_199070.

Banerji, Rishabh. "These Are The 13 Families In The World That Apparently Control Everything." *Indiatimes.com,* India Times, 9 Mar. 2018, www.indiatimes.com/culture/who-we-are/these-are-the-13-families-in-the-world-that-apparently-control-everything-from-politics-to-terrorism-257642.html.

Berkowitz, Adam Eliyahu. "Ancient Jewish Sources Indicate Trump Will Pave Way for Third Temple: Prominent Rabbi." *Breaking Israel News | Latest News. Biblical Perspective.,* Breaking Israel News | Latest News. Biblical Perspective., 22 Mar. 2018, www.breakingisraelnews.com/104682/ancient-jewish-sources-indicate-trump-will-pave-way-for-third-temple-prominent-rabbi/.

Beyer, Catherine, et al. "Deists Believe in One God Who Is Impersonal." *Thoughtco.*, Dotdash, www.thoughtco.com/deism-95703.

Challenge, World. "AN URGENT MESSAGE." *English - World Challenge Devotions Blog*, Blogger, 7 Mar. 2009, davidwilkersontoday.blogspot.com/2009/03/urgent-message.html.

"Encyclopedia Judaica." *Suleyman*, www.jewishvirtuallibrary.org/court-jews.

Farberov, Snejana. "All Presidents Bar One Are Directly Descended from a Medieval English King." *Daily Mail Online*, Associated Newspapers, 5 Aug. 2012, www.dailymail.co.uk/news/article-2183858/All-presidents-bar-directly-descended-medieval-English-king.html.

Flynn, Mark A. *Forbidden Secrets of the Labyrinth: the Awakened Ones, the Hidden Destiny of America, and the Day after Tomorrow.* Defender, 2014.

"Founders Online: Old Mistresses Apologue, 25 June 1745." *National Archives and Records Administration*, National Archives and Records Administration, founders.archives.gov/documents/Franklin/01-03-02-0011.

Haden-Guest, Anthony. "How Debauched Was The Hellfire Club?" *The Daily Beast*, The Daily Beast Company, 11 Apr. 2015, www.thedailybeast.com/how-debauched-was-the-hellfire-club.

Jefferson, Thomas, et al. *The Jefferson Bible: the Life and Morals of Jesus of Nazareth, Extracted Textually from the Gospels in Greek, Latin, French & English.* Smithsonian Books, 2011.

"Johnny Depp: 'When Was the Last Time an Actor Assassinated a President?'." *NBCNews.com*, NBCUniversal News Group, www.nbcnews.com/pop-culture/pop-culture-news/johnny-depp-when-was-last-time-actor-assassinated-president-n775881.

LOCKWOOD, INGERSOLL. *Baron Trumps Marvellous Underground Journey*. 12TH MEDIA SERVICES, 2018.

Lockwood, Ingersoll, et al. *The Prophetic Works of Ingersoll Lockwood: Baron Trumps Marvellous Underground Journey & 1900; or, The Last President*. Mockingbird Press, 2017.

"Memetics." *Wikipedia*, Wikimedia Foundation, 24 Dec. 2018, en.wikipedia.org/wiki/Memetics.

O'Brien, John Anthony. *The Faith of Millions*. Our Sunday Visitor Press, 1938.

"Oil in the North: Moses' Blessing Coming to Life." *The Jerusalem Post | JPost.com*, 27 Feb. 2018, www.jpost.com/Christian-News/Oil-in-the-North-Moses-blessing-coming-to-life-543719.

"One Messiah Or Two? – Grace thru Faith." *Grace thru Faith*, gracethrufaith.com/ask-a-bible-teacher/one-messiah-or-two/.

Pike, Albert. *Morals and Dogma of the Ancient and Accepted Scottish Rite of Freemasonry: First Three Degrees*. Martino Pub., 2011.

"Ron Paul Says U.S. Has Military Personnel in 130 Nations and 900 Overseas Bases." *@Politifact*, www.politifact.com/truth-o-meter/statements/2011/sep/14/ron-paul/ron-paul-says-us-has-military-personnel-130-nation/.

Schochet, J. Immanuel. "Appendix II." *Jewish Traditions and Mitzvah Observances*, 19 Jan. 2004, www.chabad.org/library/article_cdo/aid/101747/jewish/Appendix-II.htm.

Schultz, Colin. "Why Was Benjamin Franklin's Basement Filled With Skeletons?" *Smithsonian.com*, Smithsonian Institution, 3 Oct. 2013, www.smithsonianmag.com/smart-news/why-was-benjamin-franklins-basement-filled-with-skeletons-524521/.

Snyder, Michael. "Michael Snyder." *The Truth*, 23 June 2015, thetruthwins.com/archives/30-population-control-quotes-that-show-that-the-elite-truly-believe-that-humans-are-a-plague-upon-the-earth.

"The Creation of the Prophet Muhammad." *Religion vs. Spirituality - What's The Difference?*, www.bibliotecapleyades.net/vatican/esp_vatican33.htm.

"THE NEW ATLANTIS." *Alice's Adventures in Wonderland, by Lewis Carroll*, Project Gutenberg, www.gutenberg.org/files/2434/2434-h/2434-h.htm.

"Washington's Masonic Correspondence." *Alice's Adventures in Wonderland, by Lewis Carroll*, Project Gutenberg, www.gutenberg.org/files/29949/29949-h/29949-h.htm.

"Who Was Albert Pike?" *WW1 - The True Cause of World War 1*, www.threeworldwars.com/albert-pike2.htm.

Made in the USA
Coppell, TX
23 August 2021

61034664R00127